Friendship

STUDIES IN CONTINENTAL THOUGHT

John Sallis, *editor*

CONSULTING EDITORS

Robert Bernasconi
John D. Caputo
David Carr
Edward S. Casey
David Farrell Krell
Lenore Langsdorf

James Risser
Dennis J. Schmidt
Calvin O. Schrag
Charles E. Scott
Daniela Vallega-Neu
David Wood

Friendship

THE FUTURE OF
AN ANCIENT GIFT

CLAUDIA BARACCHI

Translated by
ELENA BARTOLINI
and CATHERINE FULLARTON

INDIANA UNIVERSITY PRESS

This book is a publication of

Indiana University Press
Office of Scholarly Publishing
Herman B Wells Library 350
1320 East 10th Street
Bloomington, Indiana 47405 USA

iupress.org

Originally published as *Amicizia*
© 2016 Ugo Mursia Editore s.r.l., Milan, Italy

© 2023 by Claudia Baracchi

All rights reserved
No part of this book may be reproduced or utilized in any form or by any means, electronic or mechanical, including photocopying and recording, or by any information storage and retrieval system, without permission in writing from the publisher. The paper used in this publication meets the minimum requirements of the American National Standard for Information Sciences—Permanence of Paper for Printed Library Materials, ANSI Z39.48-1992.

Manufactured in the United States of America

First printing 2023

Cataloging information is available from the Library of Congress.

ISBN 978-0-253-06734-0 (hardback)
ISBN 978-0-253-06735-7 (paperback)
ISBN 978-0-253-06736-4 (ebook)

Friendship dances in the world,
awakening us to happiness.

Epicurus, *Vatican Sayings 52*

CONTENTS

Introduction: Thoughts on the Threshold   1

1. The Eyes of Friendship   8
2. The Cosmos That I Am   22
3. The Friendship between Us   30
4. The Friends of Socrates   62
5. Philosophers' Friendship   76
6. On Enmity   83
7. Friendship and Politics   103
8. Friendship and Nature   119
9. Sensing-With   131

Index   141

Friendship

INTRODUCTION
Thoughts on the Threshold

The Courage of Friendship

Addressing the topic of friendship requires a measure of courage—even a certain impertinence—in the era of Facebook and other so-called social networks. The amicable relationship is distinguished by traits like trust, fidelity, a disposition toward deep sharing, and intimacy. However, sociologists assure us that the attitude characterized by these traits was never more improbable than it is now, in this epoch of dramatic anthropological reconfiguration. These are times, moreover, in which advantages—both political and personal—are drawn from the instrumental utilization of enmity and from the spectacular manipulation of the war of all against all. But one might also say that, precisely in these times marked by the disintegration of traditional (that is, patriarchal) society, new possibilities are being unleashed for the experience of friendship over and above convenience, conventions, and institutional formulas. And it may furthermore be observed that human unreliability, in relational matters, is certainly not a modern innovation. One has only to read—and this is but one example—a few verses from the anthology attributed to Theognis of Megara (sixth century BC) to notice: "You will not know who is benevolent and who an enemy, unless you find yourself in seriously adverse circumstances. Many become dear friends besides the cup, but few in difficult circumstances."¹ And again:

> The delusion of counterfeit gold or silver can be endured, Cyrnus, and it is easy for a wise man to find out; but if a man acting as a friend hides in his breast a false mind and has in himself a deceitful heart, the god made this counterfeiting most elusive for mortals, and it is the hardest thing of all to discover. For one cannot understand the mind of man nor yet of woman, until one has put them to the test, as is customary with the beasts of burden; nor can one limit oneself to images, as in the marketplace, for appearances are often deceptive.²

In the reflections that follow, I will turn to ancient sources, and above all to philosophical texts, through which an archaic legacy unfolds, at once preserved and radically transformed. Indeed, in philosophical discourse we observe a way of receiving the heroic-Homeric tradition and keeping it alive without perpetuating it unreflectively—and in fact contesting it, subjecting it to critical examination, and thus transfiguring it. Particularly in the philosophical text, friendship will no longer be simply an institutional ritual, a tool for sociopolitical cohesion, a guarantee of solidarity between equals and the equally privileged. Instead, it will come to signify the union of those who exhibit determinate psychical and spiritual characteristics—characteristics that are as essentially irreducible to their bearers' belonging to a particular social class as they are to obsequiousness toward prestige, power, and assent to the ruling conventions in a given social order. Philosophical reflection points directly to the heart of friendship as human experience. Certainly, friendship is redefined, from time to time, in accordance with customs and cultural variables—but it touches on human becoming in its singularity, in very deep and mysterious terms.

So, conversing with ancient texts will not be a way of shying away from the task of speaking of and to ourselves, today; it will not be merely a dogmatic deference to the "classical," and even less to an archeological or archival interest. I will repeatedly turn to the ancient as contemporary. I do not say *current*, but *contemporary*: the contemporary accompanies

---

1. Theognis, in *Elegy and Iambus*, vol. 1, ed. J. M. Edmonds (London: Heinemann, 1931), verses 641–644. My translation.
2. Theognis, in *Elegy and Iambus*, verses 119–128. My translation. The parallel between the dazzle of precious metals and of human beings will be reprised in Euripides (*Medea* 516–519).

the temporary, the unfolding of time, without belonging to it, situating itself in a certain sense outside of time. Here lies its unexhausted vitality, its future. Hence, I go often to the past, convinced that it continues tirelessly to speak, with great precision, lucidity, and inspiring capacity. We should develop ears to hear it, to sense that which in the past remains unheard, to understand that the past is nothing classical, but rather the most overlooked of enigmas. One should always be slightly at odds with the world, outside of (one's) "proper" time—as Oscar Wilde used to say, ever so slightly improbable. That is, reclaiming a margin of freedom from the dictates of the current, from the chronological present with its trends and impositions.

Today, the grand sociopolitical structures (*architetture*) are trembling worldwide. More than ever before, the hold of axiological paradigms that traditionally positioned individuals, determined their destinies, and assigned them their roles and reciprocal responsibilities, is becoming uncertain. In these manifold global shifts, previously unforeseen possibilities for individual and collective becoming are unleashed. These are the possibilities about which I would like to speak. Perhaps friendship has to do with worlds that are not: that are not yet, and that should be desired all the more.

Ventures of Friendship

But why the Greeks? And why, as we shall see, the particular attention paid to Aristotle? Plato dedicated a dialogue to friendship, the *Lysis*; however, the topic is omnipresent in his thought. Theophrastus, Epicurus, Cicero, Seneca, Plutarch, to mention but a few names from antiquity, all wrote about friendship in essays or letters that have come to us only in part. These works are, in different forms, studies of love—of affection, of the joyful feeling of fellowship, of the sweetness of sharing—but also of the evolutionary perspective given by the bare fact that we are not alone on this earth. However, it is in Aristotle that we find reflections on friendship of unprecedented depth. Aristotle considers friendship comprehensively, exploring every aspect of its vast phenomenology: friendship between individuals (between different types of individuals, with different horizons and purposes), and then friendship as solidarity and political cohesion, friendship in its relation to justice, and, eventually, friendship as a belonging to the world and as cosmic bond. It is a hitherto unmatched synthesis, above all in the centrality attributed to the topic. Friendship will never again be given such prominence, nor ever more be captured in all its implications.

Aelred of Rievaulx (twelfth century) writes a short manuscript (*Spiritual Friendship*) in which a detailed elaboration of Christian teaching fuses with an overall reference to Cicero. Augustine and Aquinas strive to find a role for friendship and all the concomitant forms of love in Christian life. But friendship's bond, impassioned and exclusive, fits poorly with the universalistic thrust of Christianity, whose project and aspirations were reflected instead in the valorization of fraternity.[3] Writing on friendship, Michel de Montaigne (1580)[4] and Francis Bacon (1597) both seek to delineate the traits of friendship between excellent individuals (always male in gender), distinguishing it from erotic attraction, from the bonds of blood and clan, and from the universalist egalitarianism that is the mark of Christianity. Friendship would be differentiated from these by being elective, freely chosen, and irreducible to environmental, conventional, or institutional pressures.

Afterward, the topic of friendship suffers a conspicuous loss of prestige. Thomas Hobbes enters the scene of the Western world and promotes an innovative vision of human nature: the human being is, in its essence, solitary, dangerous, brutish, only contractually constrained to contain itself in order to consent to a sustainable communal life. As in the ancient saying attributed to Plautus, *lupus est homo homini*, the human being is a wolf to the other human being.[5] This perspective is therefore one already known in antiquity, but, as we shall see, Greek thought, especially with Plato, inoculates antibodies to neutralize this anthropology, or at least to render it questionable and therefore not presumed. Even for Francis Bacon—who still approached the theme with characteristic dryness, devoid of sentimental or moralistic embellishment—the human being who does not know how to relate to another as a friend must be seen as an aberration. Whoever so lives takes their character "from the beast, and not from humanity";[6] their solitude is miserable and unhappy; for them, "the world is but a wilderness."[7] This condition is so

---

3. See Lorraine Smith Pangle, *Aristotle and the Philosophy of Friendship* (Cambridge: Cambridge University Press, 2003), "Introduction."
4. Michel de Montaigne, "De l'amitié," in *Les essays* I.28. The essay was republished posthumously, with the incorporation of the notes Montaigne appended to his own manuscript, in 1595. "Of Friendship," in *The Complete Essays of Montaigne*, trans. D. M. Frame (Stanford, CA: Stanford University Press, 1966).
5. Plautus, *Asinaria* II.IV.495.
6. Francis Bacon, "Friendship," in *The Works of Francis Bacon*, vol. 12, ed. James Spedding (London: Longman, 1858), 166.
7. Bacon, "Friendship," 166.

far from defining the human in its essence that, Bacon adds, "those that want [for] friends to open themselves unto are cannibals of their own hearts."[8]

But what Bacon describes—by his own admission, in such dark tones—becomes in Hobbes the human phenomenon as such: not a deplorable exception, but the norm. The latter's vision of human nature enjoyed an unparalleled development and adherence, in modernity, and was successful to the point of appearing obvious, and thus inconspicuous, until it disappeared altogether as an object of scrutiny and critical reflection. Still in Freud, this is the conception of human nature. What prevails is the emphasis on selfishness, on individual interest, and on a calculus of personal utility: the spirit of economic liberalism, whose first axiom is the individual cut off from the environment that brought him or her into being. Unable to recognize bonds and debts of provenance, the individual experiences collectivity as a poorly tolerated limit: the society of repressed cannibalism.

Rousseau constitutes an exception in this context. Returning—as Hobbes also did—to a mythical state of nature, he postulates the human being in its spontaneous and uncorrupted goodness, empathy, and meekness. He lingers on love considered as a free relation, an expression of affinity and recognition, glimpsing in the institution of the family the place of emotional education (and experimentation). And yet, despite Rousseau's interest in the experience of affective bonds, their political and public significance comes to be completely lost in modernity; indeed, lost is the capacity to grasp the public and the private, ethical and political, in their indissolubility. In modernity, friendship comes hence to be relegated to a private and contingent sphere, stripped of its vaster systemic implications. Likewise for the mystery of love's alchemy, in part locked up in the familial institution and in part (as Nietzsche observed) codified in the most unattainable idealization.[9] On the public level, in civil coexistence, the referential paradigms are not the amicable or the amorous, but rather the fraternal—that is to say, the equality of Christian ancestry, and, eventually, human rights and universal values (as, for example, altruism based on duty). Moral law (Locke, Kant) is a mark of this progressive abstraction.

---

8. Bacon, "Friendship," 170.
9. Friedrich Nietzsche, *Morgenröte. Gedanken über die moralischen Vorurteile* (1881), paragraph 503. *Dawn: Thoughts on the Presumptions of Morality*, trans. Brittain Smith (Stanford, CA: Stanford University Press, 2011).

The conception of the human as rapacious by nature, and then citizen by culture, by training, by renunciation, but never by choice and intimate correspondence, is thus to be seized in the opposition between egoistic interests and ascetic altruism. Civilization's (that is, culture's) discontent, of which Freud writes, entails precisely this vision of the essentially repressive community, founded on the sacrifice of individual liberty. In a scenario arranged in such a manner, the feral nature of the human being could only be hypocritically mutilated and masked. There is no space to recognize the human as inscribed in a whole, interdependent, plural, and communitarian in its very essence.

And yet the ancient conception of the *anthropos* shows that there is neither contradiction nor incompatibility between my interest and that of others, between egoism and altruism. For the human being so understood, friendship is the ground of every relational register and variation. It is where the singular being may realize itself, where the sense of solidarity may take place, making togetherness cohesive. And it is here, in this concrete, lived, singular experience, that universal development is rooted.

Universalism is not a modern Christian invention; the ancients are well aware of the perspective "according to the whole," but they come to it by a completely different path. Modern universalism emerges out of abstraction—that is, out of the separation from heterogenous and irregular phenomena, in the distance that levels out and makes uniform. For the ancient experience, on the other hand, the universal arises out of an amplification of the horizon—that is to say, in a gaze that, having become more capacious, contemplates singular phenomena, grasping at once both their irreducible differences and their connections, their overall weaving. So conceived, universality articulates itself on an experiential background— it maintains contact with the concreteness of lived experiences, which are always different and mutable, yet still seen in their togetherness. It thus becomes possible to understand relationality—being in communion and in community—not as a snare or straitjacket for singularity, but as a resource. The individual, it could then be said, cannot be reduced to the posture of modern individualism. The latter reveals itself, in fact, to be dangerously illusory; rather than exalting autonomy, it cleaves and separates; more than liberating, it renders closed and fragile.

Friendship considered *more graeco* offers unexpected conditions for overcoming the supposed dichotomy between egoism and altruism. It suggests that staying together is not something to be tolerated begrudgingly—by contract, with resignation—but a pleasure, and a possibility for self-realization. And, above all, rather than a limit to my individual freedom, the other, the others, "we," are what makes possible my own being, are constitutive of my being who I am, precisely the singular individual that I am.

The reflections on friendship that follow outline thoughts, visions, stories—because, as Hannah Arendt wrote to her friend Mary McCarthy on May 31, 1971, "One can't say how life is, how chance or fate deals with people, except by telling the tale."[10] And, as is always the case in reporting voices and telling stories, it would be good not to be too certain whether these concern things that "really" happened, or were "merely" dreamed, imagined, carried within oneself.

---

10. Hannah Arendt, *Between Friends: The Correspondence of Hannah Arendt and Mary McCarthy, 1949–1975*, ed. Carol Brightman (New York: Harcourt Brace, 1995), 295.

1. THE EYES OF FRIENDSHIP

A Certain Look

Before all else, it will have been a matter of look. Subtle, inexplicable, elusive in its essence and origin, friendship is first of all, and in its most elementary sense, a way of looking, a way of bringing the eyes to bear on the things of the world. Nothing more—but also nothing less. Friendship is not a project, not a contract, not an intent—not even a yearning. It has the levity of a miracle;[1] like a miracle, friendship seems to irrupt into the order of the world and of necessity, casting it into disarray. It suspends the law according to which my thriving would be detrimental to yours, and demotes it to a prejudice. It is tenacious, creates relationships that are stable

---

1. Simone Weil, *Amitié: l'art de bien aimer,* ed. Valérie Gérard (Paris: Éditions Payot & Rivages, 2016). This short text is included in *Formes de l'amour implicite de Dieu,* handed by Simone Weil to Father Perrin in May 1942, before she embarked for the United States. *Formes* was posthumously published in 1950, in the volume of collected essays and letters *L'attente de Dieu.* The theme of friendship is pervasive in Weil's thinking, as is evident in "L'*Iliade* ou le poème de la force," in *Les Cahiers du Sud* 230–231 (December 1940–January 1941), and in the conspicuous body of work on ancient Greek thought and poetry. Domenico Canciani and Maria Antonietta Vito edited a collection of her writings and correspondence on this topic, enriched by a preface on Weil's years in Marseille (1941–1942): S. Weil, *L'amicizia pura* (Rome: Castelvecchi, 2013).

and trustworthy, cares for togetherness, and is thereby world-making. It brings the world to life, with firmness. Friendship draws together the manifold, making it unitary; it conjoins the different and composes it into an organism: "In friendship, all things contribute to the one."[2]

Complexity, as much in its immense musical scores as in its most minute expressions, seems to presuppose friendship. As a philosopher, Empedocles is capable of a wide gaze; and, as a physician, he carries the suffering of every mortal. Hence, he grasps friendship in its work, at once celestial and terrestrial—as a principle of cosmic unity (the bond of friendship characterizes "that from which proceed all the things that were, that are, and that will be"), and as the connection between and among single individuals ("friendship comes to be also in mortal limbs, so [the mortals] have affectionate thoughts and perform loving acts").[3] In friendship, things gather together and accresce; in discord and hatred, they break apart. Between these extremes are drawn the cycles of cosmic life and of ephemeral life, in a time of boundless amplitude or in the evanescence of a day.

So, the look. The ancients say that the eyes are the most luminous organ, since they themselves are full of light. Seeing means letting this inner light shine out from the eyes to meet the glow of the world, to meet the things that light up and appear.[4] And so it is that even sight, the sensory modality that projects itself further than all the others, is elucidated on the basis of the simplest and most immediate of the senses: touch. Seeing means: two lights touch one another.

Each sensory channel is a mode of contact and union with the world: an exchange in which, at the same time, we come out of ourselves and let the world enter into us.[5] From the absolute proximity of touch, to taste, which touches the solids and the liquids brought to the mouth, to smell, which touches the aromas in the air, to hearing, which touches the vibrations of the air, to, finally, sight, which touches lights, both near and farther, the different modes of sensation are but variations of a pervasive openness to the world. But sight allows us to cover the maximum distance: inner light pushes out to the most remote regions, to the lights that adorn the vault of the sky. There, it meets the ultimate limit. Over and

---

2. Empedocles, 17.7, 20.2 Diels-Kranz. Unless otherwise noted, all translations from Greek and Latin are mine.
3. Empedocles, 21.8–9, 17.21–22 Diels-Kranz.
4. Plato, *Timaeus* 45b–46a.
5. Aristotle, *De Anima* 416b32–418a6, 424a17–b18.

above the celestial bodies ("those most shining")[6]—their rhythm, their score—lies untouchable and incalculable darkness.

But what does friendship have to do with sight? In what sense would friendship be a certain way of looking, a way in which sight alights on things, encounters them and, touching them, lets itself be reached and touched in turn? A story that Plato tells us sheds light on the matter.

A Myth

It is a story (a *mythos*) about the genesis of the world, of the entire cosmos[7] (we might have to employ broad strokes, but we will try to be concise). It should be said—and this is no mere detail—that this is a story inside a story: the narration of the cosmogony is, in its turn, inscribed in a narrative context that sees the interaction of four interlocutors: Socrates, Hermocrates, Critias, Timaeus. It is the scene of a gathering among friends who are celebrating their being together according to the laws of hospitality and of reciprocal giving.[8] The word "friend" appears as early as the first line, to signal that we find ourselves within a genuine theater of friendship.[9] And, once again, a fact must be highlighted: those we find here are quite improbable friends. Suffice it to recall that one of them, Hermocrates, is the Syracusan general who victoriously drove back the expedition of Athens in Sicily (414 BC). After the catastrophic defeat of the Attic city-state, Hermocrates was without a doubt a *persona non grata* for the Athenians—and yet here we see the public enemy welcomed as a friend and honored according to the custom of respect toward the stranger. What Plato stages is evidently a friendship so capacious as to transcend considerations of alliance, identity, and political affiliation, to the point of admitting (and honoring) even the antagonistic and destructive element.

Émile Benveniste has masterfully analyzed the archaic language of friendship, deepening its institutional range—in particular, its connection with hospitality.[10] Besides its dimensions of intimacy and domesticity (which include affectivity, corporeity, kissing, *philema*), friendship designates a nexus of customs and comportments related to the welcoming of

---

6. Aristotle, *Nicomachean Ethics* 1141b2.
7. Plato, *Timaeus* 29d, 30b.
8. Plato, *Timaeus* 17b.
9. Plato, *Timaeus* 17a.
10. Émile Benveniste, *Vocabulaire des institutions indo-européennes*, vol. 1 (Paris: Les Éditions de Minuit, 1969), 87–101, 335–353.

the foreigner, *xenos*. It therefore overlaps with hospitality, precisely as law, agreement, or binding commitment: the stranger is hosted, and it is by virtue of being a guest that the stranger becomes a friend. In this sense the friend is by definition the stranger—the extraneous received *chez soi*, into oneself. But the fact that it is the gesture of hospitality that inaugurates friendship brings us back, once again, to its miraculous, exorbitant character: since the hosted stranger, treated as a friend, can always, in the extraneity of one whose nature is unknown, be the enemy. With respect to the unknown, with which there is no acquaintance, calculated risk is impossible—only absolute exposure. Hospitality reveals friendship in the dazzling light of trust. Without calculation, one entrusts oneself to the undecidable possibility of both friendship and enmity. In the face of maximum risk, in the face of the guest who might reveal him- or herself to be hostile, friendship stands vulnerable, defenseless but trusting.

It is thus that friendship arises, in the heart of foreignness, turning to the outside: it seeks relation, solidarity, not so much with those who are close, but with those who come from afar. Even before designating the deepening of intimacy and familiarity (*consuetudine*), friendship is the name of an openness to the unaccustomed (*inconsueto*). It dares to interrupt the automatic equation between the stranger and the enemy, and at the same time opens a fissure both imaginative and propitiatory, risky and adventurous. One will never have reflected sufficiently, with sufficient wonder, upon this fact.

The hosting ones lend themselves to becoming hostages to the guest(s),[11] offer themselves to those who do not belong in the community, as if dimly aware of the vulnerability, of the exposure involved in non-belonging, in being so far away from anything customary. Thus is friendship initiated. Although rarely observed outside of Homeric exegesis, it must be said that loving, offering friendship, means belonging. Belonging is one of the meanings of the language of *philia*, above all in its verbal and adjectival forms. *Phileo se*: I am fond of you, I belong to you. In establishing this relationship with the stranger, one comes to belong to them: one makes space for them and becomes theirs, even before being (perhaps, it is not certain) reciprocated. The one who does not belong—who belongs neither to me, nor to the community—is the one to whom I belong, the one to whom we belong. One belongs to the friend who comes, unknown. One belongs to the relationship, launched as a bridge

---

11. Even "hostage" refers to the etymology of hosting, of the host (*hostis*).

between us. It is thanks to this relationship that one is who one is, and that the world opens up. No wonder, then, the inclusion of the foreigner in the formula of the happy life, according to Solon: "Blessed the one who has young friends and solid-hoofed horses, hunting hounds and a guest from afar."[12]

On the opening scene of the Platonic text, we should limit ourselves to these brief annotations. So, how does Timaeus tell the story of the generation of the world? He says that the demiurge ordered what already was there and moving in a disorderly way. That is, the demiurge brought to light, and so defined, the nebulous matter with which he was working, and without which he could not have started anything.[13] Too human, this artisan god: bound to matter for his work, without option of creation *ex nihilo*. The matter is already there when he sets himself to work; he merely intuits its potential. He sheds light on an order that in the primordial matter is only implicit, a trace.[14] And it should be observed that this image is already significant for our topic: the demiurge works through recognition and persuasion—that is, he seeks the agreement of matter, tries to convince it to unite with him in a creative task. Matter is neither violated nor manipulated as an inert and indifferent resource, but rather comes to be understood in its possibilities and approached in the mode of an exchange. In an essentially harmonizing approach—that is, tending to unite the different—matter comes to light, although it is never resolved into light.[15]

Conferring order means giving life. That is how the great, living body of the cosmos is born: spherical, gathered inside the furthermost sky in which orbit the fixed stars—those which, from our terrestrial observatory, do not change position with respect to one another, and compose constellations adorning, like jewels, the night that envelops us. And here, within the great sphere of what remains firm and identical, is the orbit of the different and the mutable in which move those celestial bodies that do not maintain the same positions with respect to one another, and that in fact wander, moving in a manner both irregular and surprising, if not

---

12. Cited in Plato, *Lysis* 212e. See also Ivan M. Linforth, *Solon the Athenian* (Berkeley: University of California Press, 1919), 131.
13. Plato, *Timaeus* 30a.
14. Plato, *Timaeus* 53b.
15. Heraclitus, 123 Diels-Kranz. *Physis* (the force that emerges, that comes to the light) loves radical alterity, loves hiding. Indeed, emergence *belongs* to concealment.

completely disordered.[16] These luminous bodies are, indeed, the planets, which move like nomads scoring the sky, with different velocities and even apparent inversions of course—sometimes approaching until they join, then distancing to find themselves opposed to each other, and so on for every other angular relationship. So is drawn the structure of the *psyche* or soul of the world. In the intertwined orbits of the identical and the different is the life of the cosmos, what makes it living and animate, organically composed, intelligent: an organism connected with itself, traversed by currents that propagate incessantly and convey themselves all around.[17] The universe thinks and thinks itself, senses and senses itself, perceives intellectually and sensibly.[18] And it is a friend to itself.[19] So composed, fruit of the artisan god's mastery and bounty (and of the unnamable female partner), the cosmos has a beginning but will have no end: in its perfection begins a life of infinite duration.[20]

But now there is a new problem. The living cosmos would not be perfect if it lacked imperfection. It therefore becomes necessary, in order to complete the work, to add incomplete life—finite and mortal—to what has hitherto been shaped.[21] The body of the whole must be populated with partial, irregular, caducous bodies. The demiurge, who can only create fullness and perfection, assigns this task to his divine offspring—that is, to the celestial bodies he has placed in the sky in order to make visible and radiant his mathematics. These therefore prepare themselves to create fragile life, capable of suffering: all the beings that, once born, begin to belong to death. To produce these bodies, the demiurge's offspring use the material out of which they themselves were made: every mortal, having borrowed star-matter for their own life, will return it in death.[22] And death will at one point occur because the bonds and joints with which these minute bodies are held together are neither stable enough,

---

16. Plato, *Timaeus* 36c–d, 38c–d.
17. What is here evoked in broad strokes is analyzed closely in John Sallis's luminous discussion, *Chorology: Of Beginning in Plato's* Timaeus (Bloomington: Indiana University Press, 1999). I should also mention Peter Kalkavage's translation of Plato's *Timaeus*, with remarkable introductory essay and appendices (Newburyport, MA: Focus, 2001).
18. Plato, *Timaeus* 37a–c.
19. Plato, *Timaeus* 32c.
20. Plato, *Timaeus* 34b, 37c–d, 38b–c.
21. Plato, *Timaeus* 41b.
22. Plato, *Timaeus* 41d.

nor sufficiently enduring, and with time they will loosen to the point of dissolving. Death is exactly that: the disintegration of the organism, its progressive return to its unbound, inert components, which will then be used anew in successive cycles of generation.[23]

Yet, in this mortal exiguity an immortal seed will be implanted. The demiurge does not participate in the construction of these beings, but he nevertheless makes available the principle from which he forged the living cosmos. He takes what remains of this principle—obtained by mixture, and mathematically articulated—and subdivides it into souls, which he delivers to the gods, his offspring.[24] The mortal bodies produced by them, in their finitude and vulnerability, will be bearers of souls identical in substance and form to the soul of the world. They will therefore be spherical, like the whole cosmos and the stars: small cosmoses corresponding to the great cosmos, little bodies corresponding to the great body. And—although only briefly, intermittently—they will live of the same life.

So it is that the human being arrives on the scene: us. But a spherical body can hardly manage its tasks in an adequate way on earth, given the asperity of the terrain and the cavities in which the sphere may end up, unable to extricate itself (here the Platonic theater is also a comedy, a smile-generating tactic). It then becomes necessary to furnish the sphere with a body elongated into limbs, as support, such that it can move and grasp things. The human is literally a star who walks on the great body of the earth—a star carried on a cart, or a vessel, through the paths of this life—equipped, then, not with simple and uniform circular motion, but with locomotion of a totally different kind, in six directions: up and down, right and left, forward and backward. With a characteristically stumbling gait, this new animal begins to pound upon the terrestrial surface. And in this way, too, its soul does not remain simple, spherical, constituted out of the intersection of the two circular orbits (the identical, the different); but rather becomes composite: a tripartite psycho-somatic system that consists of desire (abdomen, stomach, sexual organs), ardor (the heart and chest-region), and, of course, speculative capacity (the head, the sphere).

Gaia, the earth, is nevertheless not a fixed and unmovable abode. On the contrary, in the experience of birth and becoming, the human being

---

23. Plato, *Timaeus* 42e–43a.
24. Plato, *Timaeus* 41c–d.

is as though caught in the current of a turbulent river, overwhelmed by its erosive and consuming force. And so its supporting structure comes to be constantly disrupted, disordered, deformed, to the point of being mortally disfigured.[25] Gaia is also Rhea, and flows, vibrates, shaken by seismic movement. So, how can the human being live without being prematurely undone? How can it survive the blunt action of the world, at least for the time that it is given? And above all: how can it protect the integrity of a maximally unstable composition, of this psycho-somatic complex (desires, passions, intelligence) that, exactly because it is not simple, is always exposed to the insidious risks of schism, to the possibility of breaking into pieces?

One Sky

Having wisely arranged this background, Plato proceeds to draw out some consequences. Two of these matter for us, here, and both concern the human being's situation in the cosmos, and its safety—that is, its possibility of dwelling, of staying for a while and not simply being swept away by the often unexpected movements to which it is exposed. The body, Plato recounts, should not abandon itself to inertia but should always take care of its movement. It should feel alive, feel the vibration that runs through it, that fluctuates across it and unites it (the animal belonging to the earth and to the sky) with the vicissitudes of the other living beings and, eventually, to the vast movements of the cosmos, itself also an animal. This means that its movements will not be arbitrary, but neither will they be geometrical or mechanical.

The body will find its rhythm; it will navigate through the changing waters of life, seeking to accord with them. Far from trying to dominate and regulate the fluctuations inside and outside of itself, it will need to come to know them. Further: it will have to follow them, *imitate them*.[26] Here lies all the difference between mortality and malady: in the attempt to harmonize with the environment of which one is a part, looking out for its indomitable influences and moving together with them.[27] This makes the animal alive and life intense: no longer is the animal consumed, beaten about hither and thither like a dead body, but it participates in the pulsation of the whole. In this way, imitatively, the micro-body of mortal

---

25. Plato, *Timaeus* 43a–44b.
26. Plato, *Timaeus* 88d.
27. Plato, *Timaeus* 90c–d.

becoming accords with the macro-body of cosmic becoming. That "in which" the becoming takes place, Plato calls *chora*.[28] *Chora* is not only relentless, destructive flow, but also vital movement. Like Gaia "of the ample breast,"[29] *chora* opens up the space of life and protects it. It is vessel and nurse to every generation. The body benefits from imitating its rhythms.

But Plato also tells us: not only the body-vehicle, but also the orbits of the mind (the head) will have to be cared for, so that they may be healed of the traumas that dent them, and may have their cycles restored. Here, too, it will be a matter of connecting to the world-system and arranging oneself in imitative disposition. The human being in the great river will have to connect to what is distant, to reach, through the most agile of perceptual leaps, the farthest, infinitely distant regions of the cosmos. Surprisingly, it is still the senses that permit this extreme amplification of oneself and of one's consciousness: hearing and sight—but in particular the latter.[30] Plato says: they will have to lift their gaze, look at the sky. That is, raise themselves from their immediate concerns, from horizontal life, lived head-down. Looking at the sky, mortal life is reinvigorated, regenerated in the contemplation of vastness; the human grasps its position in it, sees beyond itself, beyond the human itself. It looks at the sky and feels looked at; in this crossing of glances (*horao*), it encounters divinity (*theos*). This is the primordial sense of *theoria*.

But this is, above all, an experience of mirroring: looking at the sky, the human being sees itself, it is reminded of itself. It had moved away from itself, caught in the incessant rapids of affairs that worry humans. But here, precisely in turning to this most remote and wonder-filled spectacle, it recovers itself, recognizes itself, and this is how the orbits of thinking and sensing are reconstituted in it and recover their originary configuration. It is as though the immensity to which the human opens itself would, in turn, open passages in it, making the human spacious, giving it ampler breath, reuniting the splendor of the sky with the invisible depths of which the human being is the bearer. It is here that visible and invisible touch, spilling into one another. The visible penetrates the invisible; the invisible reflects outside itself. At the center of this chiasm, the human being understands itself to be an inhabitant—not yet and not only of this or that

---

28. Plato, *Timaeus* 49e.
29. Hesiod, *Theogony* 121.
30. Plato, *Timaeus* 47a–c.

city, this or that region: a citizen of the great work, it inhabits the world. Here, perhaps, lies a possibility for approaching, if not thinking through, the enigmatic meaning of the visible imitation of the invisible.

Unlike the earth, which we meticulously partition and claim as property, the sky is everyone's. It is maximally open, undivided and communal: everyone under the same sky, which is one.[31] The Pythagoreans—and Plato with them—used to say that things belonging to friends are held in common.[32] And Heraclitus, illuminating the other side of the matter, lamented the all too widespread tendency to settle on the narrow perspective of the private, of self-referentiality devoid of connections.[33] Looking at the sky, I recognize myself, and the memory of my essence is awakened in me. But my essence consists in my self-overcoming: overcoming myself toward the other, in every direction. So, looking at the sky I do not see myself *only*, but myself as *us*. I see that in which everyone, just like me, is reflected. The sky, in that way, reminds me that I bear *us* in me: I bear in me the community as a destiny of sharing, and also as a provenance. That is: I carry others upon me; I am therefore responsible for them, because I carry others within me constitutively. Of others, by others—this is that of which I myself am made; and that is why I understand them, why I feel their feelings—why I perceive, even confusedly, their sufferings, elations, visions, and efforts. I undergo (*patisco*) these with them, and I recognize myself in their vicissitudes.

Here we have friendship in its most elementary sense—and most elementary, here, means even more difficult, to the point of unattainable. Friendship arises in a way of looking, of being touched, of receiving: in a look of particular luminosity and awareness. And it is not fixed in an abstract formula: this sense of friendship is rooted in the living experience of commonality, where what is held in common are not so much properties or attributes (what one is, what one has, what one knows), but shortcomings and inadequacies (what one is not, what one does not have, what one does not know). We share a condition that is precarious and full of pitfalls, we face trials and hardships without being prepared for them, we pass through life exposed in all our fragility. I am a wandering

---

31. Aristotle, *Metaphysics* 1074a31. See also Giordano Bruno, *The Ash Wednesday Supper*, trans. Stanley L. Jaki (Paris, The Hague: Mouton, 1975).
32. The phrase *koina ta ton philon*, ascribable to Pythagoras, is dear to Plato. See Plato, *Republic* 424a, *Lysis* 207c, *Phaedrus* 279c, and *Laws* 739c; Aristotle, *Nicomachean Ethics* 1168b8, as well as Cicero, *De Officiis* I.51.
33. Heraclitus, 1, 2, 89 Diels-Kranz.

star, a star of unpredictable movements, and I roam in the company of many like me.³⁴ Even Aristotle observes that it is precisely this *pathos* that builds the radical sense of community, the dawn of friendship: "In travels, too [ἐν ταῖς πλάναις], one may observe how close [οἰκεῖον] and dear [φίλον] every human being is to another." And he adds that for this reason friendship "seems to hold a *polis* together [συνέχειν], too, and lawgivers seem to pay more attention to friendship than to justice."³⁵

Planetary life—in its wandering sense (*planein*)—brings us together. In the course of a journey, human beings tend to regard each other with understanding and sympathy. *Syn-patheia*: they are all exposed to the same *pathos*. Precisely in facing dangers and uncertainties, wandering through unfamiliar places, humans feel more than ever the closeness between them. Those who meet each other along the way, who travel part of the road together, or who simply cross paths, recognize each other as neighbors—that is, as similar. *Oikeion*, Aristotle says, to underline a condition that brings us closer to the unknown and makes us feel its familiarity. Hence closeness is not collocation in space, and similarity should not be understood as superficial conformity. The journey reflects the human venture as such: as seafarers, restless nomads, human beings plow through life; they know that endless dangers are an integral part of their terrestrial transit; they share the same vulnerability toward the immeasurable and the nonhuman. This is why they are dear to one another. *Philon*, Aristotle says of one encountered in wandering: we perceive him or her as a friend, we feel a sense of belonging, such a sight delights us. Whence the *regard*, the *respect*, words through which the visual root shines: *spectare*, looking, regarding (*guardare*), contacting the other by turning the gaze to it, building a bridge in its direction. Anyone who has traveled alone, and at length, in remote—even inhospitable—places, knows this experience. Friendship would originate precisely from the element of solidarity in the encounter: seeing and being seen, and touching, being touched. It is already here, in this communion of sensing, in this sensing-with (*con-sentire*), that the community arises, a concordant community, a community in accord with itself.

This, then, is the look at the heart of friendship: a unitive force, a capacity for seeing the bonds and holding together (*syn-echein*) the elements that form every living organism, whether a single mortal individual, human communities and those of other mortals, or, finally, the

---

34. Plato, *Republic* 614b–c.
35. Aristotle, *Nicomachean Ethics* 1155a21–2.

community that includes all of them and that is thus not human, is in-human—that is, irreducible to the human and to the mortal. Friendship sustains cohesion, makes it beautiful, seeks harmony in it, even there where it is a matter of belongings that are disturbing, disruptive—of bonds with unfathomable alterities that do not allow themselves to be brought back to a connection, or recomposed in any way.

We can now better understand the improbability (and the unheard-of availability) inherent in the opening scene of Plato's *Timaeus*. Even the archenemy is included in the amicable bond. The vision of friendship in play, here, is situated at this level. Common participation in the whole, the memory of me and of us: every enmity, every apparently irreconcilable difference, every conflict, every rejection and aversion should eventually be brought back to the recollection of this background truth. We all belong to the same sky. Awakening to this fact, disarming and unassailable, radically changes the perspectives: the vault of the sky that looms over us, and watches us, protects even the incompatible. No exclusion. This is why the image of the cosmos that Plato elucidates—in the *Timaeus* just as in the *Republic*—is, in one sense, an image of perfection and balance, harmony of the worlds, and hence, accomplished friendship. But, in another sense, it is often a matter of incalculable harmonies not ascribable to a rational order, to an order mathematically pacified and deprived of dissonances: around the axis of light that sustains the whole are composed unaccountable movements and persist impervious relations. Even that which appears to be more refractory to these reunions—that which rejects, which does not attract—is woven into the whole. And this refractoriness comes as such to be linked to all the rest: somehow joined, but preserved in its reluctance.[36]

Delicate Ways

In itself, belonging to the whole is not a philosophical novelty. It enjoys absolute privilege in the archaic imaginary of myth, especially in the context of matriarchal traditions. Here, the priority of the vital compound requires, for its success, the sacrifice of the single individual, which comes to be absorbed as a mere feature or function.[37] Philosophical discourse preserves this primordial memory and reinstitutes its radiant imagery.

---

36. Plato, *Timaeus* 35a.
37. Erich Neumann, *Die große Mutter. Der Archetyp des großen Weiblichen* (1956). *The Great Mother: An Analysis of the Archetype*, trans. Ralph Manheim (Princeton, NJ: Princeton University Press, 1955), 279–280.

At the same time, however, the philosophical cut inaugurates a new era in which the individual is studied in its absolute uniqueness and in which friendship, *philia*, is, yes, the name of the cosmic bond, but also the name for relationships between different, unrepeatable individuals of whom one can tell only by narrating their story. To be sure, the sacrificial tendency is not altogether absent from this discourse: the *polis* tends to substitute itself for the divine cosmos as the totalizing horizon, requiring the individual to be framed in terms of the duties and roles of the citizen. And yet, far from exhausting the sense of the bond between friends, friendship as an instrument of political coherence (rituals of hospitality and solidarity, valorization of equality and equivalence, institutions of justice) is nothing but the thinnest threshold between two inflections of friendship not due to customs and conventions. Beyond this threshold (beyond friendship under the guise of political sustainability) is friendship as the total architecture of nature.[38] On the hither side of the threshold are the friends: the delight of staying together without coercion and without sacrifice. This relation fosters the formation of unassimilable, aware singularities, questioning themselves and, thus, experiencing themselves as open questions ("Who am I?") and growing in this openness.[39] It is the birth of a sense of self not sacrificed to the necessities of commonality (be it cosmic or political)—a sense of self that is not antithetical to the community, but developed within it and capable of experiencing it and encompassing it beyond strict necessity, beyond the bond that imprisons.

Friendship thus becomes the name of a free being together, of a community not so much of tolerance (one tolerates that to which one is ineluctably bound and that which one must unfortunately suffer), but of joy. In this interdependence the individual is not sacrificed, but magnified—it can be and become more fully what it is.

Hence, philosophical discourse recalls the remote mythological background: friendship as the weaving of the whole. But into this is woven the new occurrence of friendship as a free relation between and among individuals, always unique and unpredictable, as a workshop of intimacy between and among different beings, where the difference is not only admitted but cultivated, deepened. Friendship is thus composed in multiple registers: the stabilization of relations in a ritual and institutional key, the harmonization of and with the whole, the subtle nuances

---

38. Plato, *Symposium* 185c–188e.
39. Plato, *Phaedrus* 229e.

of affection and proximity between microcosms. And, precisely in holding together all of these aspects, friendship remains a perspective rich in future, in essential indications—above all for an epoch, our epoch, that progresses by simplifying through polarization and schism, forgetting that opposites belong to one another and that the reasons of the whole (*katholou*, universal) and those of individuals are not incompatible.

"Friendship," *philia*, is in every case a gentle word. Despite its ancient roots, already attested to in Mycenean Greek,[40] it has a very different destiny from *eros*. Primordial god,[41] mysterious force, mad, and, at the same time, as authoritative as a principle, *eros* has presented itself variously in divine, demonic, and anthropomorphic guises: phantasmagoria of the amorous fever. Although often woven into and contrasted with it, *philia* has never become a figure of its own.[42] It remains umbratile, indefinitely polysemic, indicating the ways of delicateness that are manifest in bonds.[43] In the final analysis, one can speak it only through a multitude of proper names, places, stories, fantasies. It has not received a visible profile, and from its invisibility it looks: friendship designates a certain gaze and, resting its eyes on things and on the world, has always already recognized a connection.

---

40. Benveniste, *Vocabulaire des institutions*, 87–101, 335–353. See also Pierre Chantraine, *Dictionnaire étymologique de la langue grecque* (Paris: Klincksieck, 1968), 1206.

41. Parmenides, 13 Diels-Kranz; *Theogony* 120–122.

42. Empedocles sometimes superimposes *Aphrodite* (or equivalent epithets, like Cypris) to *Philotes* (e.g., 17.24, 73.1, 75.3, 98.3 Diels-Kranz). Lucretius, *De rerum natura*, refers to *Venus*.

43. In the *Theogony*, Hesiod mentions *Philotes* only once and says it is daughter of Night (224).

2. THE COSMOS THAT I AM

Coming Out of Oneself

We began with a myth, and this is perhaps no coincidence. Myths convey themselves through images—they make thinking visible, shining. It is as if the words would come out of themselves to go among phenomena, among the things of the world—to clothe themselves in their appearing and thereby to speak through them. The essential trait of the mythic word is precisely this outward movement, this going outside, an external passage through masks and semblances. Crossing the landscape of the image, the word spreads itself out—it does not remain folded in on itself—and in this way it unfolds, explicates itself, cloaked in apparitions. Even when, having returned to itself, the word will pretend to be extraneous to the image, still the image will be its sense.

Is this not, perchance, the very same movement as the movement of friendship? Is it not the relation of friendship (that coming out of oneself, that going toward the other that gives each one back to oneself) that opens pathways to the most intimate knowledge, and awakens the sense of self in each one? Through the friend, I discover myself, I understand myself. But this is not a matter of mere mirroring, which in the crudest and most instrumental way would make use of the friend as a reflecting surface, as my double. The relationship with the double is another thing altogether, as shown by Narcissus's attraction, which is at once a falling into oneself and an alienation from oneself, hypnosis, abyss of the undifferentiated. No: friendship is the work of difference. Thanks to the friend, thanks to my going out of myself toward and with the other, I become a place of otherwise unimaginable openings, and I expand myself in directions that at once define me and are unforeseen by me. Friendship thus comes to signify a passage through the image, not of me, but of the other, and eventually the image of me as other than me. It is a passage through alterity (through the world that appears, exteriority, the image, the unimaginable, the faces of the other, the other without a face . . .), in which one does not aim to possess it and lead it back to oneself, nor encloses oneself in a definitive solitude.

Therefore friendship, like myth, entails an unfolding through and in images, an excessive and uncontrollable passage through exteriority: both belong inextricably to the world. But in this belonging to the visible both are always already theaters: places of vision, where one sees and is seen, where one gradually begins to see oneself, beyond every predictability. In this regard, we are reminded of Hannah Arendt's reflections on the political sphere as the place where human beings convene without coinciding, constituting a plurality. The properly political space is the space "between" human beings, thanks to which they can manifest themselves (each one singularly, with all the concomitant risk and unknowns), demonstrating "who" they are through their (com)portment and their undertakings. It is a space constitutive of the human as such—that is, of the human as capable of conscious action (*praxis*) and speech (*logos*). It is here that the human being practices that which is most proper to it. It is here that human (hi)stories develop, interweave, mirror, and reflect one another—and give each other back to one another; and it is in their constant and reciprocal confrontation that they take note of themselves, apprehend themselves, and seize their trajectory and the possibility of returning to themselves.[1]

For Arendt, then, it is in the theater of the *polis* that the invisible of each individual comes to visibility, and humanity explicates itself in an ever new becoming. As we shall see, if it is the *polis* that makes human fulfillment and realization possible, in deeds and words, friendship appears as a privileged place of this elaboration and experimentation. Indeed, it is in the experience of friendship that the conditions for the

---

1. Hannah Arendt, *The Human Condition* (Chicago: University of Chicago Press, 1958), chapter 5, "Action."

intensification and perfecting of human potentiality are given. Aristotle says that it is in friendship that human beings are more than ever able to be.²

The Hidden World

And yet . . . and yet, Plato, once again, complicates the landscape that is only barely becoming delineated. And perhaps this helps us to see better—or rather to perform an acrobatic movement with the gaze, which disposes us to the invisible. It is a matter of shifting our gaze from the landscape of the cosmos to the cosmos that each of us is, from sidereal distances to the endless expanses of interiority. But saying that each one of us is a cosmos means, once again, understanding that each one is many—and that this multitude is neither a mere quantity, nor a crowd, but a composition, an organization of disparate and therefore uncountable, not numerable elements: a highly unstable organism, worthy of wonder and study. The gaze thus scans the invisible and discovers it to be no less vast, no less mysterious. And this transformation, this revolution of the gaze, by venturing into the invisibility of interiority, makes it possible to intuit further dimensions of the experience of friendship.

In particular, friendship should also be understood as a relation with oneself, as a prerequisite (or as an equiprimordial condition) for friendship toward any other being. We find this argued for most clearly in the *Republic*. This is no coincidence: the *Republic* is a dialogue that gravitates around the question of justice neither as juridical-legal precipitate, nor as abstract essence, but as an arrangement of the soul. And, since the soul is that whose task is to live (the text adopts an extreme minimalism in this definition),³ the question concerning justice will not so much ask "what" justice is as such, but rather how life could be when justice dwells in it: what it might be like to live and act (to be) according to justice, with and in justice, in a just configuration. Hence, the question regards justice in life, in the soul;⁴ and this, says the text, independently of whether the justice of a life transpires in the world or remains hidden from it, whether it may have witnesses or not, whether it may be verifiable or not, recognizable or unrecognized, publicly honored or misunderstood, even vilified or persecuted. In other words, the question is: Is it worthwhile to be just,

---

2. Aristotle, *Nicomachean Ethics* 1155a16.
3. Plato, *Republic* 353d.
4. Plato, *Republic* 358b.

even if one receives condemnation or abuse as a result? Is it worthwhile to be just, even in the most austere solitude? Plato poses this question in the most intransigent—which is also to say, the most demanding—way.

The issue of friendship is therefore situated within a meditation on the just life. This research proceeds from a hypothesis that imposes itself as the only access to the invisible: the isomorphism of *psyche* and *polis*. Because the *psyche* is, for us, unfathomable in itself, we will delineate its structures on the basis of those of communal life, where each *psyche* manifests itself in action, allows itself to be seen in its bearing and behavior with respect to others. It is on this basis that the well-known parallel tripartitions of the psychic and political organisms are elaborated, in which it is important to understand the qualitative dimension of the number *three*. If *one* is the absolute, self-comprehending unity, if *two* is the movement with which the one passes from simplicity to an incipient but still indeterminate differentiation (which cannot yet be counted or defined), *three* is the first number. It indicates a multiplicity in which differences begin to be discernible and therefore countable. Thus, *three* is as much the cipher of the human being (*psyche*) as of the institution of human coexistence (*polis*), both of them being complex entities, articulable and analyzable into their components. We should recall this when we discuss the "three parts" of the *psyche* and of the *polis*. Here, unity must be understood as the place of difference. And difference is, therefore, not equivalent to separation.

As concerns the *psyche*, and specifically the phenomenon of life in human form, the following are acknowledged as components of it: desire in all its guises and implications (instinct, impulse, creativity, destructiveness, urgency . . .); the variant of desire that burns (as fire always does) upwards (passion, dedication to a task, the impetus that sustains a project);[5] all-encompassing vision (*theoria*)—that is, the ability to connect, to see links, to articulate (*logos*, *logismos*). It should be observed, once again, that *psyche* is the name of the whole somatopsychic complex, and is in no way opposed to the body: the body is in fact part of it, as shown by the inclusion of the appetitive and instinctual elements. In Platonic discourse, then, the individuation of the virtues (of the excellent operative modalities) corresponding to the three functions follows from this analysis of psychism. It is thus said that, at their best, desire is expressed in the finding of a

---

5. *Thymos*, to which is connected the name of the gland above the heart, in the upper part of the chest, indicates the ability to adapt and to respond to the world, in the struggle and in the defense of life.

measure (moderation), ardor in courage, and all-encompassing vision in wisdom.[6] And justice?

Justice comes into play precisely at this point, as a fourth and unexpected excellence: unexpected because it does not correspond to the exercise of one psychic function, and therefore interrupts (or complicates) the triadic logic of the psycho-political system. The intuition of something like justice emerges out of the elucidation of the *psyche*; it is evident in the way the *psyche* has been brought to light: justice is what comprehends and grants the excellent exercise of each of the three functions. According to its principle, each "part," each element, each one, should do what is proper to it, what belongs to it.[7] This means, at the same time, setting to work each difference as such, and protecting each from the others' interferences and invasiveness. Doing what belongs to each means not assuming nonpertinent functions—that is, not disturbing the others' activation and exercise, compromising their integrity, provoking confusions and disorders, absolutizing certain activities to the detriment of others. At the psychic level this occurs, for example, in dependencies (be they affective or physiological), when desire dominates, uncontested, and claims for itself the initiatives and capacities of the other components, thereby crushing the life of the whole individual, confining it within the scope of a totalizing desire that has become obsession and torment. Or it happens in repression, when a rigid and dogmatic rational function wants to impose itself on the impulses, disowning them and violating them. In every case, the individual is thereby impoverished. Disorder (the usurpation and assimilation on the part of one function over the others) restricts life. It renders life less varied, less differentiated, less nuanced. And furthermore (this is even more disquieting), it throws life into disarray, exposing it to the risk of scission: when the functions reciprocally disturb each other, their cohesion, the possibility of their coordination, of a peaceful and creative juxtaposition of neighboring constituents, dissipates. And life becomes one-sided, unbalanced.

Hence, justice is a practice of differentiation, a tutelage against fusion and meddling. And this is what guarantees synergy. Justice thus becomes the name of an order that, far from sterile rigor and mere procedure, is the structure of life itself: the name of a constructive principle—or, better, a generative one—that promotes the union of the different, protecting both unity and difference, and so favors ever more complex

---

6. Plato, *Republic* II–IV.
7. Plato, *Republic* 433a–b.

aggregations, the development of connections, growth. The gaze (the contemplative and connective function) comes to be essential in this sense: it observes, it safeguards, and thus maintains, sustains. Opening itself to the other than itself, not closing itself off in a self-referentiality unable to see beyond itself, is indeed a distinctive trait of vision; it is no accident that the broad range of the contemplative capacity is a cipher of wisdom.

But contemplation and its correlation with *logos* (as *logismos*, the capacity to discern, evaluate, relate) are burdened by interpretative automatisms that enjoy the utmost prestige in the transmission of philosophical discourse. On their basis, contemplation comes to be read in a hegemonic and repressive key with respect to the other dimensions of the *psyche-polis*, as a cipher of violent and debasing domination.[8] So, it is opportune to insist that at play in contemplation is neither restrictive control nor abusive power, even less submission of the irrational part to the rational, but rather a gaze that makes itself a guardian and steward. If there is a hierarchical privilege conferred on the contemplative factor, it is because this element, precisely by being what it is, can become the guarantor of coexistence, of composition, of a unity of different functions. But this unity, to repeat, is nothing uniform—it does not sacrifice differences, but, on the contrary, saves them. This, desire cannot do; confined in itself, in its cravings, it can only seek its own satisfaction, no matter the cost. Ardor, passion for a project, is already more capable of looking beyond itself. But it is in the gaze, in contemplation, that this self-overcoming, which is a mode of transcendence, can be most fully enacted. Desire does what is proper to it: it *desires*, and in doing so it simply affirms and replicates itself, always self-same. The gaze, too, does what is proper to it: it sees, and seeing is always already going beyond itself, beyond the mirror and beyond infinite self-refraction. Seeing is always seeing other than oneself, and holding it together—seeing the togetherness, manifold and yet gathered, co-operating.

In all the ways Plato images the *psyche-polis* or *psyche*-world system in its tripartition, it is never a matter of eliminating, invalidating, or even merely shaming the desiderative, instinctive, corporeal dimensions—in

---

8. This exegetical perspective is common to the most reductively dogmatic philology and historiography as well as their detractors and critics, starting from Nietzsche's challenge against "Christo-Platonic" moralism. This is the unspoken, unthought common ground (and commonplace) of both logocentrism and its deconstruction.

short, *eros*—because these are the dimensions of pulsating life, of motion, and of generative motivations: the horses that pull the winged chariot in the *Phaedrus*, the torso and limbs on which the head rests in the *Timaeus*, the creators in the *Republic* (those who work the land or who, in various ways, produce works of ingenuity, and own all riches and material goods), are the living root of any further construct.[9] But cultivating these elements is essential (all the attention of the philosophical gaze is turned toward this task) so as to transform their always possible destructiveness, so as not to compromise the possibility of growth in complexity. Even Aristotle repeats this same gesture, in ways all his own. When he distinguishes excellence from mere continence, Aristotle, like Plato, underscores the fact that continence (self-restraint) is nothing but an impoverished expedient. Continence is the expression of the mode of reason that wants to curb instinct or desire, forcing it to heed reason's advice. But excellence consists not in forcing but in cultivating, the tireless work of formation. It is harmonization between reason and the power of desire: a harmonious convening of both, so that it is no longer a question of forcing anything, of violating or of showing proof of force. Here again, this term that we have already encountered many times, that has inconspicuously been part of our conversation since the very beginning: harmony.

In the *Republic*, as we have already seen, justice results from the harmonious interaction between different components; it is the excellence of a unity in which difference as such becomes visible, and is accordingly interconnected and preserved. In the text, this is also called friendship. When the various psychic elements are in harmony among themselves, each exercising what is proper to it and, at the same time, each well connected to the others, the individual is a friend to itself.[10] In the somatic-psychic complex a mode of relationality is actualized that is the same as that which holds together the multiple notes in a chord: each of them, as different, is linked to the others, and all of them together contribute to a more comprehensive unity. Such is the harmony spoken of by the Pythagoreans.[11] It would be impossible to underestimate the therapeutic potential of friendship with oneself, of the care for inner harmonization, if it is true that the individual, far from being indivisible, is a unity dynamically

---

9. Plato, *Phaedrus* 245c–257b, *Timaeus* 42e ff., *Republic* 372a–b.
10. Plato, *Republic* 443c–e.
11. Simone Weil, *Amitié: l'art de bien aimer*, ed. Valérie Gérard (Paris: Éditions Payot and Rivages, 2016). The sense of harmony is at the heart of Weil's interpretation of Plato and the Pythagoreans, see paradigmatically Simone Weil, *Intimations of Christianity among the Ancient Greeks* (London: Routledge, 1957).

implicated in the play of differences, always exposed to the possibility of "falling to pieces." The human is indeed a highly volatile compound, always on the verge of self-forgetfulness and dis-integration; unstable as the wind in all its degrees of intensity: from breeze to hurricane, from gentleness to brutality, from warmth to polar winter . . . And, moreover, care for interior accord is of absolute importance, if it is true that friendship with others is unthinkable apart from this elementary sense of friendship.

As in friendship as cosmic bond, and as in friendship as a bond between individuals, likewise in friendship with oneself it is essential to include the most disruptive elements—those that we would be least inclined to acknowledge and to admit: listening to oneself, opening up to the understanding even of one's shadows, of those contents experienced as insidious, negative . . . healing the war within, soothing, bringing about peace, perceiving oneself as the bearer of conflict and disharmony within, and providing care on the basis of such experiences. Fundamental texts from classical psychoanalysis and from analytic psychology, from Freud to Jung to Erich Neumann, are extensions, albeit in transformed circumstances and languages, of this line of reflection.[12]

The good life implies this harmonization inside and outside: the friendship that embellishes my life with the beauty of fellowship, and the friendship that cures internal bonds, and hence the integrity of the system that I am. In each case, the phenomenon of friendship belongs to the tendency toward the good, of which, in the Platonic text, justice is the precursor and announcement. Friendship is love of the good and manifestation thereof. The good (at the same time, the good of each and the good common to all) motivates and requires friendship. So say the Greeks. But what does it mean?

---

12. The process of elaboration is the keystone of Freudian thought in its comprehensive trajectory: working through, and therefore transformation of denied and potentially destructive motives (from mourning, to trauma, to conflict). See, paradigmatically, S. Freud, "Zeitgemäßes über Krieg und Tod," in *Imago. Zeitschrift für Anwendung der Psychoanalyse auf die Geisteswissenschaften* IV (1915). In Jung, one should indicate the theme of the shadow, gradually developed from the individual psychic dimension to the supra-individual and collective one. See C. G. Jung, *Wandlungen und Symbole der Libido* (Leipzig: Deuticke, 1912), revised as *Symbole der Wandlung* (Zürich: Rascher, 1952), furthermore *Psychologie und Alchemie* (Zürich: Rascher, 1944), *Antwort auf Hiob* (Zürich: Rascher, 1952), *Mysterium Conjunctionis: Untersuchung über die Trennung und Zusammensetzung der seelischen Gegensätze in der Alchemie* (Zürich: Rascher, 1955–1956). This line of reflection is brought to its extreme consequences by Erich Neumann, *Tiefenpsychologie und neue Ethik* (Zürich: Rascher, 1949).

3. THE FRIENDSHIP BETWEEN US

The Intensity of Life

The considerations on friendship as solidarity between and among different elements, and therefore as a guarantee of the greater constancy of every compound (of each and every organism, from the mortal individual to the entire cosmos), should not induce us to neglect friendship as an exquisitely human relational phenomenon. And, in the task of reflecting on such matters, Aristotle is an unmatched point of reference. No one, either before or since him, has explored with comparable subtlety and breadth the different forms of friendship in their ethical, political, formative, and spiritual implications. No one has drawn such attention simultaneously to the affective and sensible dimensions of friendship, and to its visionary, even utopian, implications. Friendship seems to be, for him, a matter of inexhaustible interest. To stay with his most celebrated text in the ethico-political sphere, it suffices to recall that of the ten books that compose the *Nicomachean Ethics*, two are wholly devoted to the analysis of this topic. Aristotle does not devote such extensive consideration to other subjects.

Aristotle underscores the absolute necessity of the friend for a good life—that is, a happily realized one. Friendship nurtures our blossoming and delights us. The pleasure it brings is absolute: it cannot be brought back to an ulterior end. Friendship therefore turns out to be essential and extreme, an expression of excellence ("friendship is an excellence, or something with excellence"). And besides, "more than any other thing," friendship is "most necessary to life," and in fact "no one would choose to live without friends, even though they would have all the other goods."[1] Friendship's indispensability for exploring and realizing human potentiality is sharply underlined: "Friends help the young in guarding them from error; and the old who, because of their weakness, need care [θεραπείαν] and additional support for their actions; and they help those in the prime of life to do beautiful actions, as in the saying: 'And two are going together,' for with friends human beings are more able [δυνατώτεροι] to think [νοῆσαι] and to act [πρᾶξαι]."[2] Obviously, at stake is not merely survival, the sustaining of biological life. Hereby another necessity is announced, a necessity no less necessary than the conditions for subsistence. The human being lives presaging a surplus of unfathomed possibilities, a margin to explore. Well exceeding biological survival, the human being has a sense for the beyond as its vital and necessary element, and hence demands it; and, probing it, realizes itself. The superabundance of the possible is inscribed in its experience. It is, for the human, necessary.

Friendship, in its various guises, allows us to see this clearly: the human being is presented, characteristically, as open to that which is not yet, projected into a becoming that is a discovery and realization of potentiality. Just as, in the circumstances in which one can lay down one's arms, one can enjoy relief and a freely expansive motion, so in friendship one finds a privileged place in which to be. Friends assist and encourage each other in their various vicissitudes, in focusing their action and thought, in experimentation and in research. For this reason Aristotle observes that, precisely thanks to friendship, human beings are more capable of becoming fully what they are, of realizing their potential. The amicable bond greatly favors those who are touched by it: with this support, friends can each confront the task entrusted to them, which consists in living in such a way as to activate their whole being, and therefore in an act accompanied by reason, or, more broadly, by the exercise of thought. This reflective being in the world (living according to *logos* or not without *logos*, says Aristotle;[3] living the examined life, says Socrates[4]) is exactly what the Greeks mean by virtue or excellence.

---

1. Aristotle, *Nicomachean Ethics* 1155a4–6.
2. Aristotle, *Nicomachean Ethics* 1155a13–16.
3. Aristotle, *Nicomachean Ethics* 1097b38–1098a20.
4. Plato, *Apology* 38a.

Aristotle cites the *Iliad* ("When two go together, one discerns before the other"): there, it is Diomedes who exalts being together in an enterprise, since the capacity for incisiveness, lucidity, and concomitant resources (*noos, metis*) are thereby enhanced.[5] The operations of war become more effective: in the Achaeans' hour of anguish, Diomedes and Odysseus will go spy on the enemy's camp. Having captured Dolon, the Trojan spy, and having obtained information from him, they will surprise the sleeping Thracians, massacre them, and take away their horses. The usefulness of going together is here graphically concrete. But beyond strategic missions crowned with success, shedding light on human potentiality means revealing the human being as surprising, unpredictable, a source of wonder. An example of this is the case of Damon and Phintias, two friends and followers of Pythagoras.

Their legend, reported by Aristoxenus of Tarentum—and retold by Cicero, Diodorus Siculus, and Iamblichus, among others—portrays the vision of friendship in the Pythagorean and Platonic traditions.[6] It recounts how the two friends found themselves in Syracuse during the reign of Dionysius II. Accused of plotting against the tyrant, Phintias was condemned to death. Phintias then asked to be able to return home, before the execution, to settle his affairs and take leave. After some hesitation, Dionysius accepted, on the agreement that, if Phintias would not return by the agreed time, his friend Damon would be executed in his stead. Damon's trust must have seemed to the tyrant both touching and naive, so willingly did Damon offer himself. At the appointed time of the execution, as Damon was about to die, Phintias returned, having been delayed by various mishaps along the way. But then the tyrant, full of astonishment and admiration for the completely unexpected proof of fidelity, spared his life, and (surely to the disappointment of Pythagorean detractors) asked the two friends to be admitted as a third member to their friendship. Iamblichus feels the need to specify that the tyrant's wish could not, by any means, be granted, but, in any case, the function of the tale is clear: it celebrates the wonder of friendship, at once characterized by extreme openness and therefore vulnerability, and by an unprecedented potency that renders it invincible, irresistible, contagious.

---

5. Homer, *Iliad* X.224–226.
6. Cicero, *De officiis* III.45; Diodoro Siculo, *Bibliotheca historica* X.4; Iamblichus, *De vita pythagorica* 33. See, too: Valerius Maximus, *Factorum et dictorum memorabilium* IV.7. ext. 1.

Friendship is thus intimately linked to the possibility of setting to work the potential of human beings as human beings. For this reason, it corroborates, strengthens, amplifies, and emphasizes. In other words, still: friendship is the condition and context for the utmost explication of human *dynamis*. There is freedom in this. There is joy, intensification of life. There is a willingness to offer help and therapy—where "therapy," according to the meaning of the Greek word *therapeia*, does not designate a cure like an orthopedic device, a corrective remedy, but is rather a practice of offering service, of assisting, of honoring: one honors the friend in the way in which one honors divinity, taking care of what one brings to the celebration, of gifts and festivities.[7] This is the pinnacle of humanity.

Among the most accomplished evocations of the sphere of friendship is Plato's *Symposium*. There, friendship is celebrated as something adorning life, as a necessity over and above the necessities dictated by survival: as an altogether other order of necessity. Here, the friends join together to feast with their guest, Agathon, the playwright victorious at the Dionysian festival. But excelling in theatrical art means knowing how to ignite vision, inducing mirrorings and refractions between action on stage and in life, and hence stimulating consciousness of oneself and of the world. Friends thus gathered do not share only delicacies that entice the palate, but also another form of nourishment: a certain freedom from that which is strictly necessary, with the concomitant sense of lightness, flourishing, and expansion of horizons. And so, after eating and drinking, they stay up late talking—simply for the pleasure of talking. Friendship is a way of staying together that is different from the contiguity of animals grazing in a pasture or near the coolness of a spring on a summer day.[8] Aristotle as well underlines the difference between the living together of human beings and the grazing of animals; although later (in a development rich in consequences, as we shall see in due course) he will proceed to underline the sharing of sensation in friendship—that is, the possibility of perceiving being (being there, being alive) with the senses, of savoring together the bare fact that one is, and how sweet it is to be, how sweet the being there of the other, being together.[9]

---

7. Plato, *Phaedrus* 255a. Valerius Maximus, too, compares the veneration due to friendship to that due to divinity, noticing that in both what is at stake is to guarantee health—that is, well-being, safety (*Factorum et dictorum memorabilium* IV.7. ext. 1).
8. Plato, *Phaedrus* 259a.
9. Aristotle, *Nicomachean Ethics* 1170a27–1170b19.

So, we stay together not only to organize, to feed ourselves, to face together the indissoluble constraints of necessity, but for the pleasure of mutual company. It is a necessity of a completely different nature: a human need to go further (above all, beyond oneself) and, in this disclosure, to discover what would otherwise be unattainable. Friendship nourishes extraordinary developmental possibilities.

The Forgotten Good of the Other

With Aristotle, we could say that the word "friendship" can signify many things. Many relations that come to be called by this name are in fact instrumental relations, motivated by various ends (pleasures or interests of different genres, the acquisition of material goods, projects . . .). But how does friendship appear in its full sense—a friendship we would call complete, and therefore perfect?

We should not hear, in Aristotle's talk of perfection, a reference to the ideal, but rather friendship as an end in itself, a bond neither reducible to a means for determinate ends, nor established in view of obtaining anything. It does not lead to any end, if not the good, which is not itself a thing: friendship is oriented to the good of oneself and of one's friend. But being an end in itself and aiming at the good means, for friendship, the same thing: being the place where nothing is pursued other than full realization—that is, happiness, mine and the other's. Hence, an accomplished friendship is the accomplishment of everyone.

The principal requirements of friendship are similarity—or affinity[10]—and reciprocity.[11] But, straightaway, it should be said that these terms indicate neither conformity, adaptation to convention, nor quantification and calculation. Similarity, here, does not mean belonging to the same social class, and, likewise, reciprocity is not reduced to calculability, hence it is not inscribed in the economy of giving and taking. Friends do not resemble each other merely in some marginal detail, in outward forms, or in the sharing of the same benefits and privileges. And what they give to each other is not measurable in the way of an exchange of ordinary goods—it is not a quantity to which a price may be assigned. Between friends, similarity and reciprocity are rather understood in light of a propensity for excellence, for the perfecting of life: *arete* is the name

---

10. Aristotle, *Nicomachean Ethics* 1156b8.
11. Aristotle, *Nicomachean Ethics* 1155b34.

the Greeks give to this existential posture, usually translated in English as "virtue."[12]

So, common to friends is the form of life, the way of living—both in invisible interiority and in the exteriority of action. It is the disposition toward the good, the good of life—that good that is life itself striving for accomplishment, for joyous fulfilment. In friendship, the interweaving of the present good (the friend's excellence), and of the good as a tendency, infinite task, good to come, is maximally magnified. Aristotle observes that "the perfect friendship is between human beings who are good and similar with respect to virtue; to the extent that they are good, they wish the good for each other, and such human beings are good in themselves."[13] At the heart of this friendship is the sharing of excellence and the mutual wish for ongoing growth and completeness. And it is precisely the movement toward the good (that which makes one excellent in *psyche* and in action) that is eminently amiable and attractive in the friend. Friendship, then, is this community, this originary commonality, essential and in constant development.

Some of the implications of what we have been saying must be underlined. To be sure, friendship means favoring the other's becoming. Aung San Suu Kyi stated, in her acceptance speech for the Sakharov Prize, that in the work "to realize our hopes and dreams . . . we do need to have friends," and friends are "those who believe in us and who want to help us, whatever it is that we are trying to achieve."[14] They are the *participes curarum* whom we consult, with whom we share our concerns, from whom we receive advice in dealing with transitions and situations

---

12. The Aryan root *ar-* is associated with dynamism, movement, solicitation; it particularly indicates intensity, focus and hence evidence, perfection, excellence (*aristos, areion*); but also loyalty, adhesion; finally, well-ordered, linked articulation (*arthron, arithmos*).

13. Aristotle, *Nicomachean Ethics* 1156b7–10.

14. Active in politics and in the promotion of civil rights in Myanmar under a military government, Aung San Suu Kyi received the Sakharov Prize in 1990 and the Nobel Peace Prize the following year. The ceremony for the conferment of the Sakharov Prize could take place only in 2013, since until 2010 she was under house arrest. As a politician in power, however, she became an increasingly controversial figure, especially from 2015 onward, due to issues such as the handling of violence against minorities (above all, the Muslim Rohingya population) and the prosecution of journalists. Her Sakharov Prize was revoked in 2020. After the 2021 coup d'état and the return of the military junta, she has been under arrest and cut off from the public sphere.

that are not easy to read. However, this not only means helping the friend in need and difficulty, but also rejoicing in their success. It is often said that the friend is the one who does not abandon us in dark times, but it is equally noteworthy that the friend knows how to be happy for us, how to be with us in bright times. Perhaps Oscar Wilde's annotation is only hyperbolic when he writes that anybody "can sympathize with the sufferings of a friend"; however, his conclusion rings deep and true: "But it requires a very fine nature . . . to sympathize with a friend's success."[15] In friendship, it is the other's good that is good for me.

Friendship, thus, evidences that which always and in any case regards us—namely, the relational (that is, always already political) character of each individual's attainment (or lack thereof). In the ancient experience it is clear that individual freedom and relational bonds are not contraposed, let alone incompatible, since the individual itself, far from subsisting autonomously outside and above the relationship, is the fruit thereof, and finds there, in relationship, the propitious terrain for its own development. That is also to say, relation is constitutive of the individual, and it is in this constitution that the individual is configured as free: not free *from bonds*, from the other perceived as an interference and a disturbance, but free *in bonds*, in being bound, in bounding and belonging with the other, thanks to the other. But this is not so evident from the perspective of modernity. We find ourselves in times of deceptive celebrations of the individual who wills itself autonomous—times in which everyone moves as if their steps, their actions, their thoughts would not have an imponderable impact on the world; as if, in turn, the world would not inform every individual in its most hidden and secret recesses; and, above all, as though no one would owe anything to anyone. But contemporary individualism does not promulgate individualism in the sense of realized singularity, but rather its caricature. Far from concerning itself with the individual, it strives to exalt empty forms of arbitrariness and egotism, which in fact make the individual ever more isolated, fragile, and manipulable, ever more disposed to believe that its self-realization occurs through the consumption of goods made available to it, ever more a prisoner of a parodic diminution of life. The logic of parody is insidious. When it becomes a hegemonic and totalizing cultural register it impoverishes, cuts, pollutes minds, dulls.

---

15. Oscar Wilde, "The Soul of Man under Socialism" (1891), in *The Soul of Man under Socialism and Selected Critical Prose*, ed. Linda Dowling (London: Penguin, 2001), 157.

It is not by chance that to reflect on friendship we must turn to other epochs; we struggle to contemplate seriousness, fidelity, and the depth that they entail, without cynicism. We tend to confuse the intensity of this experience, which is also a life project, with rhetoric. Not to mention the good, a word so crucial in the ancient experience. Everything that concerns the good arouses suspicion, for our late-modern ears—and in particular the expression *being good*. The good, goodness, good: clumsy categories, made unrecognizable by epochal upheavals that gave them back to us as inert formulas, laughable (if not altogether repressive) moralistic principles. We inhabitants of late modernity are barely able to understand what the ancients say: for them, being good means being happy, feeling disclosed in the vastness of life, seeking fulfilment, attainment in such self-disclosing aliveness. But those who came later, especially after Kant, had to learn instead that the good coincides with happiness only in God and in his infinite transcendence, while for the human being the good coincides with duty. Those who arrived later had to learn that the good entails free subjection to duty, in the most severe disjunction from the pleasure and the sweetness of being alive. Only submission to duty can hold universally. Happiness, and likewise friendship, recede into the background and do not merit further attention, since they seem to be wholly contingent, "private" vicissitudes.

We late-hour moderns, coming after Kant, have believed we could emancipate ourselves from the good as duty by turning it upside down, into a parody, precisely. But in doing so we have limited ourselves to a reactive response, remaining caught within the very same conception of the good. It is extremely arduous for us to sense other aspects, other possible configurations of the good. And for this reason, in our late epoch, terms or phrases such as "common good," "citizenship," "community" risk losing their concrete sense and their live proximity. Not recognizing the good as a realization of a *self* within an *us*, we believe we can find freedom and happiness in purely arbitrary and disconnected compartments.

Or we are connected, however not among ourselves, but to the machine—and through "the machine" we communicate globally, at this point largely sucked out of ourselves, drained, like empty shells hanging from the network terminals. But understood in this way, connectivity is a grotesque forgery of the community of friends, just as "augmented reality" is a caricature of the fullness of life.

Similarity and Reciprocity

Let us try once again to listen to the ancient discourse. Friends resemble one another in that, being similarly oriented toward the good, they pursue it, strive for it, and in this they support each other. But each one will do so in one's own way. The happy fulfillment of a life will always take absolutely unique, singular forms. So, being similar does not mean becoming the same. Friendship does not require conformism: friends resemble each other because both (or all involved, if more than two) aspire to become themselves—that is to say, to resemble themselves. Therefore, the resemblance between them is not based on traits that they possess, on properties that could be objects of comparison and comparative evaluation. What friends share is not a possession, but something that is missing and, precisely for this reason, desired and sought. They long for the good—they love it and live in the thrust toward it—and thus they love each other, and each recognizes and loves in the other the openness to loving. As Aristotle notes in the *Eudemian Ethics*, "For us" human beings, "the good is according to the other,"[16] and "each one wishes to live together" with one's friends "within the limit of the possible,"[17] especially "in the supreme good,"[18] enjoying the "more divine pleasures."[19]

One may object that the similarity between friends is based on excellence, and hence on possession, since excellence is a habit, or a constellation of habits, and therefore, in a strictly Aristotelian sense, a property, something that one "has" (the Greek noun for "habit," *hexis*, comes from *echein*, "to have"). Indeed, being excellent means presenting a certain character structure—that is, a stable configuration of habits—and this in fact can be considered a property. And yet, it is a very peculiar property: it turns the individual who possesses it toward that which exceeds the individual and toward that which the individual cannot possess. Excellence is that very particular possession that turns the one to whom it properly belongs beyond oneself—that is, beyond the very structures of possession and ownership, as well as those of property and entitlement, toward a certain expropriation. In this sense, the excellent habit indicates that the human being, in its utmost manifestation, cannot be framed in terms of autonomy, self-enclosure, and self-identity, let alone in terms of property and propriety. In its highest (and at the same time, deepest) realization, the human being displays a constitutive permeability, undergoes a determination coming from elsewhere, and becomes aware of this condition.

---

16. Aristotle, *Eudemian Ethics* 1245b18.
17. Aristotle, *Eudemian Ethics* 1245b8.
18. Aristotle, *Eudemian Ethics* 1245b2.
19. Aristotle, *Eudemian Ethics* 1245a39–b1.

Hence, friends share their disposition toward the good. They are alike in their posture with respect to the good, alike in being implicated in love for the good. This is the spur that friends share, this love that cannot be reduced to the love of one for the other. Likeness, no less than reciprocity, must necessarily be understood in light of this excess, of this openness beyond each of the friends involved, even beyond their own relationality, their tension to unite, to converge together into one. Aristotle recognizes the exuberance and superabundance of friendship: friendship is *hyperbole*, hyperbolic, intrinsically marked by excess, by a vertiginous impulse.[20] Hard not to hear, in these movements of ancient thought, the consonance with a faraway voice—that of Nietzsche—that will divine, in the relationship between friends, "a new desire and appetite, a *common* and higher thirst toward an ideal that surpasses them."[21]

One loves an other in virtue of the orientation toward the good, an orientation common to one and the other, to the one who loves and the one who is loved. Therefore, in loving the other, the one who loves recognizes oneself, in the first place, as other. And this is not only because each recognizes itself through the other, because one arrives at oneself essentially thanks to a departure toward the other, in an ecstatic movement, outside of oneself, that can never allow for a simple return without dispersion. But, furthermore, one recognizes oneself as other because in the other (and therefore also in oneself) one contemplates a further reference to alterity—an infinite openness to radical alterity, completely irreducible to another human being, to any other being, to being itself (the good, first and final principle, in Plato as well as in Aristotle, remains "beyond" every definition, exorbitant with respect to the order of the ontological).[22] The fact of recognizing oneself as other means glimpsing oneself as an open structure of receptivity and hospitality, inhabited by what is irreducible to oneself, and reaching out toward such irreducibility. Friendship thus entails sharing that which is not possessed, that which eludes possession, that which escapes and is lacking. Together, friends sense and experience the open structure that they themselves are: the open structure of incompleteness, the yearning that this implies

---

20. Aristotle, *Nicomachean Ethics* 1158a12, 1166b1.
21. Friedrich Nietzsche, *Die fröhliche Wissenschaft* (1882), paragraph 14. *The Gay Science*, trans. Josephine Nauckhoff (Cambridge: Cambridge University Press, 2001). My translation.
22. Plato, *Republic* 509b; Aristotle, *Metaphysics* 1075a11–1076a4.

and the singular orientation toward that which is *never* reduced to a surrogate or an expedient to fill in the void.

In loving the other, then, each one at the same time projects oneself beyond oneself, beyond the other, and equally beyond the relation between them. Friendship can neither be brought back to, nor contained in, the exchange between the friends alone. Since, in loving the other, one is caught in the common movement toward the good—that is, in the movement of living well, of life in its fullness (in a fullness that does not mean the inertia of an achieved satisfaction, but rather an inextinguishable desire of realization). Surely, this is what we call happiness.

Love for the friend is *at the same time* a thrust beyond the friend. In fact, this thrust beyond is as essential in the beginning as in the endurance of friendship. And such an overcoming does not signal a betrayal of the friend, but a sharing of that of which no one is proprietor or master. The freedom of the becoming of each one is found here, in this bond that does not bind to conformity. Here is the cultivation of the space between them, which is a space of nonfusion, nonfusional. Here is the distance that allows the simultaneity of reservedness and intimacy, and above all difference.

Incommensurable Equality

Let us insist: so understood, similarity and reciprocity do not lend themselves to calculation and measurement. Of course, Aristotle repeatedly specifies that friendship is between equals and is a matter of equality (*philotes isotes*),[23] reporting a saying attributed to Pythagoras.[24] And yet, set in this context, *isotes* (equality) can refer neither to parity in accounting terms (parity as adequacy and commensurability), nor to parity at the social and conventional level (parity of status, prestige, class). Being equal with respect to goodness means presenting the most intimate proximity, the most profound concordance. And nevertheless, this convergence of the one and the other proves to be fleeting, hardly objectifiable, because it does not manifest in definite forms or formulas. Indeed, goodness manifests itself in the most disparate ways, unpredictable because corresponding to ever-changing circumstances. And so, to feel equal to the other, to feel goodness as much in one's own living as in the other's, is simultaneously the most limpid perception, and also an obscure one:

---

23. Aristotle, *Nicomachean Ethics* 1158a1.
24. Diogenes Laertius, *The Lives of Philosophers* VIII.1.10.

limpid because of incontrovertible clarity, and obscure just as the character of the good, which still one *feels* one recognizes, is obscure, or perhaps dazzling to the point of blinding.

In this context, *isotes* seems to refer to the affinity of two individuals who are equal insofar as each of them activates itself, explores itself, as an open unit(y), as a research never wholly completed. In the exemplary, privileged, and favorable space of friendship, each of them can express itself to the utmost, explore the possible, assume, in the best way, the task of living, and, by living, become itself. Friends are equal in sharing the same aspiration, the same impulse, the same longing that orients them, the same openness that is not a disintegration but the perspective of an ever more capacious integration. They are equal in this sharing, yet each one can, and in fact does, achieve the most singular results. Aristotle observes that friends, from the perspective of perfect friendship, are not equal on the basis of merit or analogous calculations. In such a friendship, their excellence is the initial datum, the essential condition. This is what makes them equal. And this is what distinguishes equality between friends from equality before the law. For example, in distributive justice the allotment of onuses and honors is based on the comparative evaluation of individuals, with the aim of establishing equality through proportionality: more will be asked of those who have more, and more will be conferred upon those who deserve more. This is what Aristotle names "proportional equality." However, "perfect" friendship does not involve this type of equality, but instead "equality in number."[25] Here, each friend is one, the friends are one in front of the other, together in sharing a common desire. Each of them is one precisely in virtue of such an orientation. And their movement is simultaneously relational and transgressive because it is a movement toward another and beyond themselves.

So, pursuing the same desire may in no way mean becoming identical. On the contrary, assuming the task of living well involves confronting the question, always absolutely unique, concerning oneself, one's own circumstances, and one's singular conditions. It therefore entails developing distinctive traits and realizing the potentialities of which one is the bearer. Pursuing the same desire, then, means, for each to become itself: equal to the other and different, and above all equal in ways that one does not know how to say. Infinite and infinitely different are the

---

25. Aristotle, *Nicomachean Ethics* 1158b29–33.

paths of the quest for the good—identical in their tension and yet not superimposable, or even divergent. In the thrust of friendship lies each one's possibility of individuation, the phenomenon of each pursuing its own particular development. And individuation is not individualism, but instead each one's becoming according to its own potential. Incommensurable singularity takes shape in relation. It is constituted and develops as a place of interconnection.

Hence, the likeness and equality in play in ancient discourse do not concern particular habits or existential styles, particular political, institutional, and cultural conventions, and the reputation these confer. The relation that we are examining cannot be framed simply as the bond of convenience and conformity that unites those who enjoy the same political visibility. Nor can the community of those who aspire to the good (the community of the best, *aristoi*) be mistaken for aristocracy in the sense of the class that enjoys material advantages, power, and hereditary automatisms. Greek philosophical reflection is always resolute in reaffirming this fact: to ethical-spiritual excellence does not necessarily correspond recognition, and on nobility of soul are not necessarily conferred noble titles. In fact, for the most part this does not happen. It could be said, instead, that the relationship Aristotle calls realized friendship discloses the possibility of the individual's emergence as such, beyond functional rapports, the satisfaction of conventional requirements, the fulfillment of preestablished roles: beyond civic-political interactions and their codes.

Thus, Greek reflection (in this case, Aristotle's) cannot be interpreted and expounded within the limits of the historico-cultural context it reflects, and from which it still begins. It cannot be said that the Aristotelian vision of friendship is reducible to the relationship between two or more free, male adults—or, more precisely, between two or more citizens belonging to the dominant social class (that is, the only ones who live a life of political engagement and ease). Of course, in the context in which Aristotle lived, it was precisely these men (free from conditions of servitude and from the restrictions imposed on women) who were most likely to find themselves in a condition to experience the bond of friendship in its full sense. Nevertheless, Aristotle's thinking is not limited to reflecting such circumstances. The philosophical gaze may find its inception in precise and delimited contexts, but it also transcends them. Thinking is not reducible simply to bearing witness to one era, to one historical period, and indeed it never coincides entirely with its own time; it overflows, transgresses its own time, moves ever elsewhere, opens onto new times. That access to the amicable relationship was paradigmatically available to the free citizens (the aristocrats) coeval with Aristotle does not mean that these aristocrats automatically experienced such relationship, since the friendship in question is not based on conventional excellence (on patronymic and related attributes), but on excellence in existential comportment, mode of life. It is therefore not a class prerogative.

Irreducible to historically determinate relational and communitarian forms, of which it anyway bears the mark, Aristotelian thought sees friendship as the most favorable terrain for human becoming, as the relational commitment that, above all else, and more fully, promotes the unfolding of human possibility. The human being is thus grasped in its structural openness, in the infinite and indefinite task of turning toward the good. Far from being a question of identitarian categories (belonging to a certain class, family, or clan), friendship, precisely by shedding light on the experience of excess, questions the very possibility of identity, both in conceptual and sociocultural terms. It goes straight to the heart of the matter, interrogates me as a human being, gives me ways of lingering in the suspension of the usual surface designations: before being a citizen (or a woman, or a slave), a rich, powerful, influential man (or a servant, a subordinate), before corresponding to any category, title, or office—who am I? The excellence (or lack thereof) of my life will lie in my willingness to subject myself to this question, finding myself before myself as the most surprising of enigmas. It will lie in searching for myself, in questioning myself about how to orient myself in the often tangled passages, in the not-knowing of life. Friendship is founded on equality of desire, on the perception of the urgency of these questions. This equality is not reifiable, not definable in its *quidditas*. It is not a thing. And above all it cannot be resolved into conformity. It is in this perspective that Aristotle's reflection remains vibrant, alive, well beyond the considerations of historiographical, archeological, or antiquarian tenor.

Analogously, it should be underscored that, if what has been said so far makes sense, friendship cannot be understood in terms of competition, as if it were a noble rivalry.[26] Sharing in love of the good cannot absolutely signify competing for the exclusive favors of the beloved, engaging in an *agon*, in a contest where the prize would be the conquest of the desired at the expense of the other suitor; the good, which means living well and striving for self-realization, does not lend itself to being

---

26. Pace Gilles Deleuze and Félix Guattari, *Qu'est-ce que la philosophie?* (Paris: Les Éditions de Minuit, 1991), "Introduction."

framed in terms of scarcity and therefore of exclusion, of a conquest necessarily limited to one or a few. Rather, the good designates the task of excellent self-realization assigned to each being in its becoming, a task for which friendship provides impulse and inspiration. Because friendship means encountering an other, interacting, grasping the spectacle of the good that the other hosts and at the same time is, being attracted and open to the other in their openness to the good, and finding oneself subjected to such affection and attraction.

Stability, Fidelity, Confidence

Therefore, friends compose a similitude: friends resemble each other like poetic images that illuminate and elucidate one another. Just like analogies in poetry, resemblance between and among friends conveys itself with powerful clarity. At the same time, it reveals that similarity transpires from a mysterious ground whose intrinsic law eludes us, since it is not a question of a resemblance in exterior shapes. The conditions elude us, on the basis of which we perceive a similarity between heterogeneous and distant beings—conditions bringing about the fact that phenomena of a wholly disparate order appear intimately connected and co-significant. Homer, and this is no casual example, portrays human vicissitudes through the mirror of distant (but evidently also close) natural events: "Just as thick swarms of bees go, endlessly pouring forth from the hollow stone, and in clusters fly over the spring flowers; and many hover swinging here, others there: so the many people from ships and camps along the deep beach lined up in troops to the assembly; the voice blazed among them, urging them to go, the messenger of Zeus; and they gathered together."[27] Or he resorts to images rich in surprising undertones to hint at a concealed intensity, a secret ardor: "Like someone at the edge of a field, hiding an ember in black ash, none other being nearby, to light it again there, not elsewhere: so Odysseus covered himself with leaves and hid there."[28] Or, again, likening the wonders performed by deities to works of craftsmanship, he evokes the radiant aura that can sometimes surround human appearance, as if transfiguring it into a superhuman splendor: "As when one covers silver with gold, a craftsman instructed by Hephaistos and Pallas Athena in various arts, and brings forth graceful works: so the goddess poured grace on Odysseus' head and

---

27. Homer, *Iliad* II.87–94.
28. Homer, *Odyssey* V.488–491.

shoulders."²⁹ The poet divines implicit correspondences in phenomena apparently extraneous to each other and brings them together. He limits himself to juxtaposing two or more images, letting them imponderably produce their suggestive effects. It is from the closeness of the different images, from their being yoked together, from the tension engendered in such yoking, that sense is released, indeed, bursts forth. In fact, the two images tend to merge; in a way, they amplify each other, each revealing in the other otherwise imperceptible traits, setting the other into sharper focus; and yet, simultaneously, they come to be seen together, even as one sole image. In similitude images converge into one, as in a stereoscopic perception. *Eikon*, in the singular: with this word Aristotle designates the poetic simile.³⁰ An image, a likeness that does not signify in virtue of a reference to intelligibility, but rather in virtue of an interplay of images, shifting and fluctuating. As with symbols, here we are faced with a surprising, inexplicable freedom of resonances, with echoes that thrust into the depth of images and uncover meaning, without our being able to grasp the principle that rules the game, the law of this sympathy.

As we said, insisting on the impossibility of determining the similarity and reciprocity between friends casts light on the implicit critique to which Aristotle subjects identity structures. Neglecting or undervaluing the inaccessibility of quantification would mean understanding similarity on the level of politico-economic attributes, and reciprocity in terms of market transactions. In this perspective Aristotelian thought would be diminished (as in fact often happened) to a sterile conventionalism, uncritically conveying the pure testimony of the political-cultural lineaments of its time. This, and nothing less, is at stake in the interpretation of similarity and reciprocity.

In light of such boundlessness and incommensurability, friendship cannot be exhausted in a closed relation between two (or among a few). It is uncontainable. It always entails a sense of the common belonging in what transcends both—even what transcends the human as such, and can therefore be called inhuman (other forms of life, the infinite palette of the world). I am attracted to another because I sense in him or her the same propulsion toward a common horizon, because we love the same thing (which is no thing), beyond—not beyond this world, but rather beyond me and us.

---

29. Homer, *Odyssey* VI.232–235.
30. Aristotle, *Rhetoric* 1406b, 1410b.

Nevertheless, Aristotle is also acutely aware that this movement infinitely beyond rests on altogether finite conditions: that the experience of this driving, winged relationality cannot be lived with many others, infinitely and indifferently. On the contrary, friendship in this sense is a rare occurrence. In this connection Aristotelian thought moves in yet another direction, with striking insight, and endeavors to draw the link between friendship as a relation that can only be experienced with a few others, and the friendship that unites human beings as such and all beings, in the *polis* and beyond. As we will see shortly, Aristotle will suggest that it is benevolence (*eunoia*) that opens up the irreducibly unique union between friends to the possibility of friendship in its political valence. The benevolent attitude, lived and enacted, is the pulsating heart of perfect friendship. But this same attitude can also occur as a latent disposition—not activated, not necessarily realized in a relationship. It then becomes a possibility and a support for communitarian life in the mode of love rather than in that of a contract. We will examine this movement more closely in due course, but, for now, let us consider the finiteness that characterizes "perfect" friendship—a finiteness that cannot be explained merely by assuming the scarcity of excellent human beings.

In the types of friendship one can experience, one's psychic configuration becomes manifest. Everyone reveals oneself in one's relations: one's relations with others and one's interior bonds mirror one another. Whether in an individual human being or in a community, an isomorphism holds between interiority and exteriority—between implicit, implicated, intrapsychic dynamics, on the one hand, and explicit, extrinsic, worldly relations, on the other. This, we have already seen, is a constant of ancient Greek thought, which we are now examining in its distinctively Aristotelian version. Examining friendship in the complete sense, Aristotle concedes that "perhaps one could say that these friendships are rare, for only few are able to be friends of this nature." But the crucial question is another: "Such friendships require time and familiarity [συνηθείας]; for, as the proverb says, it is impossible for human beings to know each other well until they have consumed together much salt, nor can they accept each other and be friends until each has shown him- or herself dear [φιλητός] and trustworthy to the other. Those who quickly show the marks of friendship [τὰ φιλικά] to each other wish to be friends indeed, but they are not, unless both are dear to each other and aware of this; for a wish for friendship may arise quickly, but friendship does not."[31]

---

31. Aristotle, *Nicomachean Ethics* 1156b25–33.

At first Aristotle draws out the importance of sharing experiences, of spending time together. Friendship is lastingness, a gift of time, a gift of oneself as time. Aristotle will bestow the most vivid attention to time spent together, and, more broadly, to the temporality of friendship. But, above all, he goes on to observe how the relation of friendship is the place where character is revealed in the round. Friendship lays bare the individual and thus constitutes a most privileged observatory of the human phenomenon in its most nuanced manifestations. But one comes to this relation and to this place thanks to some indispensable traits:

> It is evident that only good human beings can be friends because of what they are in themselves, for bad human beings do not enjoy each other's company unless some benefit is exchanged. Again, only the friendship of good human beings cannot be harmed by slander; for it is not easy for a good person to trust what anyone says about his or her good friend who has stood the test of time. And it is among the good that trust and unwillingness to act unjustly and whatever else belongs to true friendship are expected without question, while in the other kinds of friendship nothing prevents those things from taking place.[32]

It is clear that friendship not only reveals character, but, in its perfection, unmistakably points to excellence, and, ultimately, encourages it. Only in the context of this relation does the expectation arise concerning the most beautiful mode of living and of acting, the most skillful way of being human. Goodness, beauty, and perfection express themselves in the most concrete qualities. Aristotle indicates the capacity to rejoice in the presence of another with no further end—that is to say, to find in the friend's company the peace that seeks nothing else, that sees neither greater good, nor further advantage. He recalls, then, trustworthiness and the capacity to trust—that is, the stability that makes one reliable, steady, trusted and, along with it, the openness that makes one confident, disposed to rely on someone else, so that one will not be easily at the mercy of slander or prey to blunders. Mutual trust (at once reliability and entrustment) is tenacious, resolute, and confers a sort of invincibility upon friendship: this is what makes its lastingness possible. As a consequence, in the end, unjust action becomes maximally improbable, since such human beings are far from contemplating interactions that, one way or another, would damage others. This is so not so much because of a mechanical and fearful

---

32. Aristotle, *Nicomachean Ethics* 1157a18–26.

observance of laws, but rather because of an intimate adherence to the demands of justice, with the exercise that this entails.

Aristotle strongly insists on the factor of steadfastness. Friendship, he says, is not easily shaken. It itself tends to the radiant firmness that it loves:

> Now those who wish the good [things] of their friends for the sake of their friends are friends in the highest degree; for they comport themselves thus in virtue of themselves and not haphazardly. Accordingly, their friendship lasts as long as they are good, and excellence is something abiding. And each friend is good without qualification and also good to his or her friends; for good human beings are good without qualification as well as beneficial to each other. And likewise they are reciprocally pleasant, since good human beings are pleasant without qualification and also pleasant to each other; for one's own actions and those similar to them are pleasant to oneself and the actions of good human beings are the same or similar [αὐταὶ ἢ ὅμοιαι].[33]

The element of stability is granted precisely on the ground of excellence as habit and exercise. This is how one sculpts one's character and fixes it into a sort of second nature. In the same way, indeed, Aristotle underlines friendship's concreteness, and thus the importance of shared time. Spending time together is essential for the most complete actualization of friendship, and therefore for its perfecting. As Aristotle repeats a little further on, "Distances do not break up a friendship altogether, but only the exercise [ἐνέργειαν] of it. But if friends are apart from each other for a long time, this seems to make them forget [λήθην ποιεῖν] their friendship. Hence one says that lack of conversation has broken many a friendship."[34] So it is that, deprived for a long time of the exercise—that is to say, of the cultivation of its energy—friendship collapses into a sort of latency, and this destroys it. It can remain like a distant echo, like the relationship that one can have with books, Francis Bacon will say: incomparable to the proximity of the friend and, to some extent, "flat and dead."

Measure and Excess

At the same time, however, these discourses prepare the way for a further consideration. Aristotle indicates that the requirement of time lived

---

33. Aristotle, *Nicomachean Ethics* 1156b10–17.
34. Aristotle, *Nicomachean Ethics* 1157b10–13.

together places limits on the number of friendships that can be formed in a lifetime. One can dispose oneself toward others with kindness, cultivate benevolence: the affection (the *pathos*) of benevolence can be manifest or latent for the one toward whom it is directed, can be reciprocated or not, and can be felt for an in(de)finite multiplicity of beings, be they known or unknown. The benevolent impulse presumes the possible goodness of these beings.[35] But if we understand friendship as a lived relation, intimate frequentation and participation in shared circumstances, well, then it designates an experience that can occur (if and when it does occur) a very limited number of times, precisely because of the finitude of human life. While, through friendship, human life opens itself to infinity, the finitude of human beings in space, in time, and in resources quantitatively delimits the actualization (*energeia*) of friendship. Human beings display neither the robustness nor the energy needed to sustain an infinitely multiplied, and ultimately undifferentiated, love: "It is impossible to be a friend to many in a perfect friendship, just as it is impossible to love [*eran*] many at the same time (for love is like an excess [*hyperbole*], and such excess is by nature felt toward one), and it is not easy for many people fully to satisfy the same one at the same time, or perhaps for many to be good at the same time."[36] The assimilation of the language of friendship to that of love (*eros*) is often disregarded by scholars, when not *a priori* denied. And yet, in philosophical discourse, and especially in Plato, it is altogether common to find the language of *philia* and that of *eros* employed alongside each other. Both relational modes entail excess—friendship no less than erotic attraction. Aristotle, who made all of his ethico-political reflections revolve around measure, balance, and composure, toward the end of the treatise, in lingering on friendship, abandons these points of reference. As if to say, having meditated on character formation and on what fosters its evolution, having reconstructed the various stages of the architecture of the human, having thus come to imagine the accomplished human being, or the way to it, behold, we must dare a step further. It must be said that a human being so constituted could transcend what has brought him or her up to this point. Having gone through the study and practice of measure, which alone confer excellence, the human can now open itself anew to the lack of measure, to a boundlessness that will not be linked to the initial condition of disorder, except in name. Indeed, the human being capable of friendship, of the hyperbolic thrust that this

---

35. Aristotle, *Nicomachean Ethics* 1155b32–1156a5.
36. Aristotle, *Nicomachean Ethics* 1158a10–14.

implies, has little in common with the human prior to the work of formation and awareness. In a certain sense, the work consists in a transmutation of excess: from structureless disorder to the overcoming of order in a movement of rapture.

As an experience of excess, friendship has something of the surprising. Let us permit ourselves a very brief digression on this subject. We are used to characterizing amorous or passionate affairs in this way, as evidently belonging to the element of fire—to its suddenness, unpredictability, and inconstancy, to its destructiveness. To friendship, we tend to attribute a more temperate warmth—balance, composure, fair distance—and perhaps it surprises us that such an analysis (*philia* as *hyperbole*) comes to us from so-called classical antiquity. Montaigne was of the same opinion: to the "feverish flame" of amorous passion he counterposed the affect of friendship, "all gentleness and smoothness, with nothing bitter and stinging about it."[37] And yet, in hindsight, he expressed himself very differently in telling of his own friendship with Étienne de la Boétie: "In the friendship I speak of, our souls mingle and blend with each other in such a universal mixture that they efface the seam that joined them, and cannot find it again. If you press me to tell why I loved him, I feel that this cannot be expressed, except by answering: Because it was he, because it was I."[38] And again: "Our friendship has no other idea than itself, and can be compared only with itself. It is not one special consideration, nor two, nor three, nor four, nor a thousand: it is I know not what quintessence of all this mixture, which, having seized my whole will, led it to plunge and lose itself in his; which, having seized his whole will, led it to plunge and lose itself in mine, with equal desire, equal thrust. I say lose, in truth, for neither of us reserved anything for himself, nor was anything either his or mine."[39] And so, in Montaigne, the hypothesis of a temperate and measured friendship unfolds and is transformed, eventually becoming a vivid example of the excess evoked by Aristotle. Similarly, the presumed separation between passionate love and amicable affection tends to dissipate, as it happens in a certain way in the ancient text. But a divergence between this latter and the modern essay must also be noticed. In telling of the "full confusion" of the "wills"

---

37. Michel de Montaigne, "Of Friendship," in *The Complete Essays of Montaigne*, trans. D. M. Frame (Stanford, CA: Stanford University Press, 1966), 137.
38. Montaigne, "Of Friendship," 139. Translation modified.
39. Montaigne, "Of Friendship," 139. Translation modified.

of friends,[40] Montaigne believed he was referring precisely to Aristotle, to whom he attributed the "definition" of friendship as "one soul in two bodies."[41] And yet, the announcement that friendship involves becoming one is not found in Aristotle: the excessive, ecstatic dimension of friendship does not imply a merging into indifferentiation. In fact, the source is rather Diogenes Laertius, who, making the formula enduringly popular, spread conviction of its "Aristotelian" ancestry.[42] And indeed, only a subsequent thinking that had learned the separability of soul and body, *psyche* and *soma*, could entertain such a conception.[43] It remains unthinkable for Aristotle—and, in general, for a thought that makes no concessions to an insensible and incorporeal spirituality.

Given the intensity that characterizes friendship as well as love, experiences of this kind occur in a limited number. This independently of the fact that, in communities as we know them, good individuals (structurally open, available to alterity and its risks) may be few or many. On this last point, Aristotle remains ambivalent. Sometimes he observes, with disarming adherence to the facts, that, indeed, excellence does not seem to be particularly widespread. Other times, he complicates things, hesitates, underlines the tension between the quantitative and qualitative acceptations of goodness: between goodness as that which can be shared in variable measures ("by some but not others or only a little") and goodness as that which can be pursued "in different ways."[44] But, in any case, all of his ethico-political reflections cannot but presuppose goodness, excellence, as potentially accessible to the human being as such, with consequent commitment to favoring its fulfilment.

It is essentially because of its hyperbolic character that friendship can be lived only according to a certain measure, a certain number of times. If this relation entails time shared, constancy, deepening, regard for the other, how many such friends could each of us ever have, in the brief life we are given, with the labile and intermittent energy we have available to us? Sharing this experience indiscriminately with many

---

40. Montaigne, "Of Friendship," 136–141.
41. Montaigne, "Of Friendship," 141.
42. Diogenes Laertius, *Lives of Eminent Philosophers* V.1.20. According to Diogenes's formulation, the friend is "a single soul that lives in two bodies."
43. Cicero, *On Friendship* XXI.81, XXV.92. Cicero presents a variant of this definition of friendship: as a mixture of two or more souls, such as to make them "as if" only one.
44. Aristotle, *Politics* 1328a36–b2.

would seem to be out of the question, for friendship is "commonality of sensing in act, set to work"—that is to say, a "sensing together" or "sensing-with" (*synaisthesis*) that should be enacted, lived in the concreteness of exchanges, and this is possible within the limits of a relation between two or "a small group."[45] Friendship so understood activates this "felt communion" that philosophers, indeed, tried to extend, as far as possible, beyond the intimacy shared by two friends, or few. In ancient philosophical communities, from the Pythagorean to the Hellenistic schools, they yearned to practice life together (*syzen*) as friends and thus to fathom unexplored human potentialities.[46]

Insofar as it ignites, empowers, and multiplies life, making it more alive, more sensitive, friendship is a potent antidote to the anesthesia that, today more than ever, ensnares minds, making them indifferent, absorbing them in a disincarnate virtuality. Indeed, as Aristotle and ancient discourse in general understood, friendship entails incarnation, and hence a capacity to feel, to sense, to traverse joy as well as, crucially, suffering and caducity. Whence comes to pass the affirmation of life. On the other hand, every idealization that alienates itself from such incarnate roots, announces the most brutal insensibility, suppresses life: it fixes life in the condition of a cut flower. In this regard, it is worthwhile to question our inclination to interpret technologically our need for ulteriority, for intensity, for fullness. We search for an "augmented," "enhanced" reality—not through perceptive refinement, work on sensibility, disciplined cultivation of attention and presence, the quest of experience, but rather through the application of prostheses and extensions to our body, ever more machine-like. To say nothing about the need for anything "extreme," like certain sports (indeed, "extreme" ones) or the use of psychotropic substances. Without any associated wisdom, awareness, or respect, we unleash the powers dormant in them, just to shake up a body already more dead than alive, and a dazed psyche.

In any case, on the finitude of human life and on limited possibilities of living amicable relationships, Aristotle inquires further. In particular, he wonders what can be said to be proper, proportionate, and adequate to the human condition, remaining well aware of the distinction, dimly illuminated, between what is possible in principle, in abstract, and what is practicable and achievable in deed. In play are the themes of measure and sustainability: the measure (*metron*) of the human, what properly defines

---

45. Aristotle, *Eudemian Ethics* 1245b23–4.
46. Plato, *Letter* VII.

human beings and allows them to manifest themselves as such, in their integrity, in the profile that distinguishes each of them. Contemplation of excellence, of the good human being, orients such considerations, for it is humanity at its best that shines greater light on the mystery of measure. Or, better yet: measure filters through with particular clarity from such humanity, from the happy life. This "is the measure," the meter. Or, so it is said.[47] Aristotle continues:

> In the case of excellent human beings, should there be as many friends as possible, or is there, as in the case of a city, a certain limit [μέτρον] of them? For neither would ten human beings make a city, nor will it remain a city if increased to one hundred thousand human beings. Perhaps a plurality has no unity unless it falls within certain limits [ὡρισμένον]. So in the case of friends, too, there is a limited plurality, and perhaps there is an upper limit of those with whom one could live together; for, as we remarked, this is thought to be friendship in the highest degree [φιλικώτατον]. It is clear, then, that one cannot live together with many friends and attend to all of them in turn.[48]

Aristotle's hesitation in drawing these conclusions is evident (the repeated "perhaps," the appeal to current opinion, to what one thinks). And yet, experience furnishes incontrovertible evidence: "It is difficult, too, to share the joys and sorrows in an intimate way with a great number of friends; for it is very likely that at the same time one will be sharing pleasures with one of them, but pains with another."[49] There seems to be an insurmountable difficulty with regard to the indeterminate extension of friendship actually lived. In augmenting the number of friends, sharing with each one of them becomes more partial, fragmentary ("pleasures with one . . . pains with another"). As previously observed, the cause of this is the finite (or, we could say, perspectival) character of the human being and of each single human endeavor. Such is the restriction to which this being is subjected—this being whose power (whose potency or potentiality), even though its confines are elusive, remains far from being absolute and all-encompassing. The experience of perfect friendship entails projecting oneself toward the incalculable (the hyperbolic), being traversed by an immeasurable movement. And it is precisely in this immeasurable experience that the human being as such is subjected

---

47. Aristotle, *Nicomachean Ethics* 1166a13.
48. Aristotle, *Nicomachean Ethics* 1170b30–1171a4.
49. Aristotle, *Nicomachean Ethics* 1171a6–8.

to measurement: measurement suffered as a limit, and yet proper and necessary to the human. The human being itself is the place of this measure, the phenomenon of measurement embodied. This becomes clearer in the experience of friendship, given that in this *pathos* of excess the human being proves to be structurally incapable of infinite undergoing.

The thrust beyond oneself and the fact of being affectively traversed (the two movements that define friendship) imply the limit that they transgress. In transgressing this limit, finitude, or measure, they restore it at the same time. This means that the individual will experience the excess (*hyperbole*) of friendship perhaps once, twice—at most a very few times in its life. Deepened is the distinction between an attitude of benevolence (*eunoia*) that amplifies itself as inclusively as possible, and friendship in its concrete and corporeal exercise. Surely, the sentiment of benevolence is no mere formality; it is not equivalent to nothing. But friendship lived in its materiality and concreteness is something altogether other.

Aristotle, however, continues with his reflection on benevolence—on one side linking it to the perfection of friendship, and, on the other, projecting it as a possible communitarian principle. This is an original synthesis, one that grasps political coexistence, human community comprehensively understood, not so much on the basis of contractual constraints,[50] but cast instead in terms of good disposition toward the other, toward all others. That is to say, at the heart of human aggregation one does not glimpse a generic and formal version of friendship, reduced to tolerance of others in the absence of something better. What animates and sustains human coexistence rather approaches the essence of friendship in its perfection, as if the rare and utterly singular experience of lived friendship could be infinitely and universally inflected. In the passage that follows, Aristotle distinguishes friendship in its practical actualization from a benevolent and friendly inclination toward others. This latter could be seen as an *incipit* of friendship, as incipient friendship:

> Benevolence, then, is like the beginning [ἀρχή] of friendship, just like the pleasure of being in love with another by sight; for no one is in love if he or she has not first been pleased by the look [ἰδέᾳ] [of the beloved], and the one who enjoys the form of a person is not by this alone in love, unless he or she also ardently longs for that person when absent and desires that person's presence. So, too, people cannot be friends unless

---

50. As in Plato, *Republic* 358e–359b, 360c–d.

they have first become well disposed [εὔνους] toward each other, but those who are well disposed are not by this alone friends; for they only wish what is good for those toward whom they are well disposed but would neither participate in any actions with them nor trouble themselves for them. Thus one might say, metaphorically, that benevolence is untilled [ἀργήν] friendship; and it is when benevolence is prolonged and reaches the point of familiarity and frequentation [συνήθειαν] that it becomes friendship, not the friendship for the sake of usefulness or pleasure, for no benevolence arises in these.[51]

Hence, the disposition of kindness and benevolent attention toward others is grasped as a precursor to friendship—as a matter of fact, as the condition of its possibility, just as the perception of enchanting features is a condition of falling in love. However, if it is not developed over time and practiced, it remains inactive, "uncultivated" friendship, a friendship in a state of *argia* (*a-ergia*)—that is, not put to work, not actualized, inoperative. Acting together constitutes the cultivation and refinement, the putting to work (*energeia*), the laborious perfecting of friendship. Yet unpracticed friendship, deprived of a definite development, remains as a principle, an orientation, an underlying affective tonality: regardless of being recognized and reciprocated, regardless of the possibility of sharing or not, benevolence desires the good of others, of those known and unknown, of those who are or who are not yet, or are no longer.

R. W. Emerson must have glimpsed something like this, when, at the end of the essay devoted to friendship (1841), he wrote, "It has seemed to me lately more possible than I knew, to carry a friendship greatly, on one side, without due correspondence on the other. Why should I cumber myself with regrets that the receiver is not capacious? It never troubles the sun that some of his rays fall wide and vain into ungrateful space, and only a small part on the reflecting planet. . . . It is thought a disgrace to love unrequited. But the great will see that true love cannot be unrequited." Why, after having contemplated unreciprocated friendship, does Emerson conclude that, at bottom, friendship is never alone, even if it is deprived of correspondence? Because friendship is, in its essence, "entireness," "total magnanimity and trust," and, precisely for this reason it cannot even hypothesize that those to whom it is addressed are inferior or unworthy. Hence, not only does friendship rise beyond the request for reciprocity, but also it assumes the excellence of the addressees. In

---

51. Aristotle, *Nicomachean Ethics* 1167a3–14.

its solar inclination, in a trusting and free way, it "treats its object as a god."[52] We will have a chance to return to these considerations, which have the greatest consequence on the political level, and which show the junction between the happenings of ephemeral individuals and those of the world.

Loving and Being Loved

A friendship sustained by a shared striving toward the good does not exclude—indeed, it comprehends—pleasure and utility. On the contrary, a relation oriented to narrowly interpreted utility and pleasures does not contemplate anything beyond these. It excludes the good beyond instrumental goods; its range is exhausted in self-referential satisfaction. Along with the inclusivity and completeness of the good as the horizon of perfect friendship, Aristotle highlights the dignity of loving and its priority with respect to being loved. In the elucidation of this topic, he touches upon the striking example of the mother, of the tenderness that wants nothing in return, the endowment that does not ask for anything but simply finds pleasure in loving: "It seems that friendship, in its very being, lies more in loving than in being loved. Mothers, who take delight in loving, are a sign of this. In fact some of them hand over their children to be brought up by a nurse, and love them, knowing that they are their children. They do not seek to be loved in return: if they cannot have both things, it is enough for them to see the children prospering; and they love their children even if these, ignoring the situation, give to the mother nothing of what is due to her."[53] The mother comes to be recognized as a cipher of a self-fulfilling affect—one that does not need further returns or benefits. That is to say, it is not an investment. It is an auspicious, patient solicitude that gives itself (when it gives itself) not through abnegation, nor through force, but through the pleasure and gratification it finds in itself. It is a love in which favoring, finding delight even just at the thought of someone, matters much more than being favored. With characteristic insistence, and returning to some by now familiar observations, Aristotle adds,

> For friendship depends more on loving [φιλεῖν], and since it is those who love their friends [φιλοφίλων] who are praised, loving [φιλεῖν]

---

52. Ralph Waldo Emerson, "Friendship," in *Essays: First Series* (New York: Vintage Books, 1990), 124. On the contrary, Augustine laments the folly of one who loves a mortal, even a dearest friend, as if they were immortal (*Confessions* IV.8).
53. Aristotle, *Nicomachean Ethics* 1159a28–33.

seems to be the excellence of a friend [φίλων], and so it is those displaying this [feeling or disposition] according to merit who endure as friends and who have an enduring friendship. And such is the manner in which unequals can be friends in the highest degree, for in this way they are made equal. Friendship [φιλότης] is equality [ἰσότης] and similarity [ὁμοιότης], and especially similarity in excellence. For the excellent ones, as such being steadfast in themselves, remain steadfast toward each other also, and they neither ask others to do what is bad nor do they themselves do such things for others, but one might say that they even prevent such things from being done; for good human beings as such neither err nor allow their friends to fall into error. Wicked human beings, on the other hand, have nothing to be certain about, for they do not even abide like themselves [in their feelings and actions]; they become friends but for a short time, enjoying each other's evil habits.[54]

The association between wickedness and instability (or uncertainty) is peremptory, in contrast with perfect friendship that, thanks to excellence, is characterized by stability and reliability. But at the core of this passage is loving, love in action. Friendly love is an equalizing factor (in loving, unequals are "made equals") and it therefore supplies the key for understanding Aristotelian references to equality: friends are equals not in respect of any particular quality, and especially not because of class and privilege, but because, independently of radical differences, asymmetries, and incommensurabilities, they love, they enact love. And then loving a friend means adopting a certain *ethos* and actively demanding it of oneself and of the other: friendship is not a lethargic compliance, an accommodating affection. It is, rather, a form of safekeeping and corroboration.

But it should be clarified that an activity such as loving cannot be understood as an act carried out by a self-determined agent—an agent who determines itself, in a voluntary and sovereign manner, regardless of the moment of passivity and receptivity. Because loving designates an act that is always already a passion. It means being caught, being enraptured by the other, undergoing a movement that is neither rationally nor autonomously determined (desire, *orexis*, remains an essential characteristic of friendship in its proper sense). We have already seen this: being enraptured by the other has at least a twofold meaning. In one sense, one

---

54. Aristotle, *Nicomachean Ethics* 1159a33–1159b11.

is attracted by the friend because in the friend one sees excellence—that is, beauty and goodness—and feels affinity, the sharing of the same desire (the same inclination toward the good). In another sense, one allows oneself to be carried away by the good itself—and the good itself (whatever this might mean) is the friend and beloved. It is therefore a rapture not simply ascribable to the attraction toward another human being. For this reciprocal attraction (this being drawn one to the other) is in its turn within the sphere of influence and tractive force of the good, which, in fact, envelops this relation and calls into play the friends who are a part of it.

According to Aristotle, what is decisive in each one's self-manifestation is less the fact of their being loved than their capacity for loving. Individual distinction resides in this capacity. Here overturned is the logic, well-known to us, according to which being loved would be more relevant and more desirable—desirable, indeed, to the point of obscuring the beauty of loving. By this logic, receiving love seems preferable, because it would confirm one's own value, it would provide reassurance about one's desirability, and so on, from delirium to dazzlement. But loving responds to a profound need and reveals who we are; it reveals us in the ongoing process of our never perfected and always singular activation: in this sense, it is easy to intuit its fundamental character. Solicited and available, the lover responds to what animates, reanimates, and enlivens them, by consigning themselves to the infinite task of living ever more fully—in the final analysis, to the task of fulfilling themselves. This task is assumed through the exercise of solicitude and of care for the beloved, as Aristotle underlines by introducing the language of the friend or lover as a benefactor, as one who confers benefits.[55]

The superior value of activating love, in comparison to being its recipient, is also decisive in facing the *vexata quaestio* of the autonomy, or even autarchy, of the good human being. Are friends necessary for such a being?[56] Let us simply note, here, that the superiority of loving to being loved does not seem merely a matter of comparative evaluation. The experience of excess, of the superabundance that leads one beyond oneself, characterizes at once friendship and the excellent human being as such. The desire to share and to give, to enact love toward the other, seems therefore to be a cipher of goodness itself. In *Magna Moralia*, we read that someone "having all good things" would need a friend "above all." In fact, about those who do not have friends, the author wonders,

---

55. Aristotle, *Nicomachean Ethics* 1167b17–1168a27.
56. Aristotle, *Nicomachean Ethics* 1169b3–1170b19.

"To whom will they do good?"⁵⁷ The sign of human excellence, therefore, will not be so much a matter of "having" (even less of having everything for and in virtue of oneself, in the highest degree of self-sufficiency), but rather of an impulse to act and to give, the joy of largesse and of beneficent inventiveness.

Oneself, the Other Self

On the basis of the presupposition of similarity and reciprocity, it is said that friendship is a sort of love for oneself: in loving a friend one loves oneself. "Being [well] disposed toward a friend," Aristotle says, "is like being [well] disposed toward oneself (for a friend is another self)."⁵⁸ Porphyry attributes to Pythagoras the formula of the friend as an *alter ego*.⁵⁹ But here one also senses the echo of Platonic teachings, which entrust intrapsychic integrity itself (that is, the harmonization of the various components of human psychism) to the unitive force of friendship, of which the *Republic*, as we have already seen, is nothing but the most programmatic expression. The Aristotelian claim above all emphasizes the reflexive position that characterizes the friend, and therefore friendship: the friend is, first and foremost, one who is related to oneself and has become a friend to oneself. In this sense, the friend is another self, *allos autos*: another one who, like me, is characterized by the capacity to turn to oneself. Another who, like me, is not only other with respect to another, but simultaneously and constitutively with respect to him- or herself as well. Being a self, therefore, means precisely this: a reference to oneself that—it almost goes without saying at this point—in no way translates into the self-referentiality of the modern subject, which wills itself transparent to itself and the owner of itself. In the most primordial sense, referring to oneself involves a mobility, or even an agility of the gaze, capable of retracing its own steps, pointing to its own provenance, and, in this movement, gathering, reassuming itself. Friendship, then, would be nothing other than the amplification of this comportment toward oneself: the transposition, at the level of relations between and among individuals, of the dynamics that ground self-perception, the perception of oneself in one's integrity, no matter how open to alterity, other than oneself, always in a process at once of becoming and dissipation.

---

57. Aristotle, *Magna Moralia* 1212b31.
58. Aristotle, *Nicomachean Ethics* 1166a31–32.
59. Iamblichus, *Life of Pythagoras* 33.

In the most comprehensive sense, friendship appears as the ground of awareness, which is always also self-awareness. In harmony with itself and nurturing the love brought about by happiness (the love of the good), as if overflowing, the individual loves outside of itself, desires the good of another and actively promotes it.[60] In fact, as the traits of this disposition belong to "someone good [ἐπιεικεῖ] in relation to him- or herself . . . friendship too seems to be some of these features, and friends seem to be those who have them."[61] It is believed that friendship has roots in a disposition toward oneself and that, therefore, it reflects one's relation with oneself and resembles it:[62] "the excess of friendship [ὑπερβολὴ τῆς φιλίας] is similar [ὁμοιοῦται] to that toward oneself."[63] For this reason, being friends with oneself does not at all mean being a self-enclosed harmony, a settled coincidence with oneself, but rather signifies the harmonious movement of a love that overflows, connects, and attunes. This friendship is the love and the cultivation of that which, even in and as me, exceeds me. All the more reason why friendship with another cannot be reduced to a process of appropriation that would assimilate the friend, rendering him or her surreptitiously familiar. The friend as "an other self" cannot mean leading the other back to myself, but instead must mean that I am turned to the other and the other pervades me *ab origine*; that, therefore, I am not in possession and in control of myself; that this relationality, this opening to the other (even to an other who is not circumscribable in the human sphere), is constitutive of what I am, of my sense of myself, and in respect of such a constitution I am always already late. I, with the capacity to pronounce this pronoun, always arrive after what is essential has taken place.

Hence, relation with oneself cannot be a matter of mastery or of unconditioned self-knowledge. Experiencing in oneself the contact with alterity, one is in the condition to love outside oneself, to recognize in others the same capacity to experience such contact and such openness to the inexplicable. Friendship with others is made possible by friendship with oneself, but also vice versa: an inner friendly disposition, self-love, the habit of alterity at the center of each of us, are fostered by the intimacy with the other encountered in the world. Care

---

60. Aristotle, *Nicomachean Ethics* 1166a1–14.
61. Aristotle, *Nicomachean Ethics* 1166a30–33.
62. Aristotle, *Nicomachean Ethics* 1166a1–2.
63. Aristotle, *Nicomachean Ethics* 1166b1.

for the mystery that I am is made possible by the relation with the friend who discloses other worlds to me and invites me to enter into the mysteries that they are. Thus, simultaneously and in an equally primordial way, all the interior and exterior paths of inquiry are opened: every intellectual undertaking, every act of reason that one would want intact and detached, objective and unaffective, is rooted in this auroral moment. Primary, constitutive, and originary, affective experience indicates a relationality that is delicate, considerate, warmly protective, and, at the same time, an *affectus* in the sense of suffering and of *pathos*, of being affected and besieged, of undergoing precisely as a passive subjection. Friendship (with oneself, with the other) always entails uncertainty, ineliminable danger, and therefore requires courage. Trustingly approaching a friend does not mean being naive, in this regard. This is why Epicurus said that one should not take friendship lightly, nor avoid it, but that "it is necessary to run risks for the love of it."[64]

That the amicable, amorous, sensible foundation leads neither to the autarchy of the subject nor to the autonomy of pure reason is also evident from the contrast between human beings and gods. This is yet another way of underscoring the limits and finitude of the human. Deprived of their involvement with others like them, human beings have no access to knowledge of themselves. Precisely because they are not gods, they can know others (and therefore become their friends) more than they know themselves. And only thanks to digression through others can they begin to access themselves. The Aristotelian discourse, no less than the Platonic one, greatly emphasizes self-knowledge.[65] And yet, while the god cannot think other than itself (its simplicity and completeness prevent it), the human being can elucidate itself only through exposing itself to another and through the other's elucidation. It is thanks to "being with" (*syzen*) that they can approach themselves, come into the vicinity of themselves.[66] The ability itself to realize difference and integrate it is distinctive of the human in contrast with the divine.[67] It is said in the *Eudemian Ethics* that, where the god, in its perfection, contemplates always and only itself, and is itself its own good, "for us the good depends on the other."[68]

---

64. Epicurus, *Gnomologium Vaticanum* 28.
65. Aristotle, *Magna Moralia* 1213a13–26.
66. Plato, *Phaedrus* 255d.
67. Hans Georg Gadamer, *L'anima alle soglie del pensiero nella filosofia greca* (Naples: Bibliopolis, 1988).
68. Aristotle, *Eudemian Ethics* 1245b16–19.

4. THE FRIENDS OF SOCRATES

A Life

But at this point we should once again consider a story: not an all-encompassing story, like the birth of the cosmos, nor the imaginative translation of the invisible, as in the vision of the *psyche*, but the story of a life, and of the friendship enacted in that life. We turn once again to Plato, because a narrator of his stature knows how to speak of the invisible as much as of the great weaving of the visible, of the immense as much as of the infinitesimal. And knows how to tell the details, the radiant vividness that belongs both to symbols and to incarnate singularity. The story is narrated in the *Apology*, and Plato has it told by the protagonist himself, in the first person. It is a story that, in the final instance, concerns the friendship between human beings (men and women), beyond the laws of the city.

Of course, it is a story inscribed in an broader sequence of events, which is that of philosophy itself in its dangerous relation with the community that hosts it. It is never sufficiently recalled that the originary scene from which Western philosophy originates is a tribunal. There is no friendship, it seems, between philosophy and the city. Philosophy is summoned before the law: in this appeal, it presents itself as fundamentally guilty, called to apologize, to defend itself. So greatly has it disturbed the city within which it was formed that it has to demonstrate the legitimacy of its existence, its right to be. Philosophy, therefore, emerges in an apology—which, in Greek, is equivalent to a speech of self-defense. The institution of philosophy—its becoming an institution, much later—will rest on the originary trauma of an accusation and a death sentence. So, philosophical activity is a matter of life and death. Of survival.

According to Plato, in his speech before the judges Socrates would have evoked the bond of friendship several times. And from this emerges a sense of friendship not only irreducible to the uses and conveniences on which political institutions rest, but also in ongoing polemic with the city. In other words, a sense of friendship in tension with a political reality that proves to be openly hostile to Socrates and an enemy to philosophy. In sketching Socrates's critical and challenging position with respect to his community, Plato basically agrees with Xenophon.

We will see, shortly, how friendship is configured in the words and gestures of the accused Socrates, but we should note an additional level of amicable activation in Plato's comportment as an author. Elsewhere, Plato tells us that the philosopher is characteristically a "friend of the ideas" and that, therefore, philosophical labor, the fruit of sharing and exchange, gives itself within the community of such friends.[1] But, then, the friends of ideas are also and fundamentally friends of one another, since it is precisely this communion that makes possible the impulse toward ideas, research into them, friendship with them. The *Apology* (the living portrait, the masterful rendering of the naturalness and ease of the spoken word, the incisiveness of the biographical episodes) reveals Plato as a friend of Socrates's even before being a friend of the ideas. Which is to say, even before what Socrates will say and demonstrate with regard to friendship, we should not miss the staging (the writing) of the Platonic theater. The text—at once testimony, poignant memory, restitution to the master and of the master—is the trace of an ultimate friendship. As always, Plato works with great reserve, tends to disappear (in the *Apology* his presence at the trial is barely suggested),[2] and yet his gesture unfolds in full light. Like Socrates—he, too, a master of dissimulation and a great illusionist—Plato withdraws to let appear that which in every way transcends him, to make sure that the ones who no longer are may live and return. It is in this immeasurable impulse that friendship and

---

1. Plato, *Sophist* 248a.
2. Plato, *Apology* 34a, 38b.

writing are welded together.³ And here friendship proves to be alive, native, courageous, creative. It promotes generation and regeneration, honors the dead, attempts the new. Overturning the judges' sentence, here Plato tells us of his friend, and shows him as the true friend of the city. A friend as true as he was unacknowledged by his own city, Socrates belongs to Athens, to the spirit of its laws.⁴ But he does not belong to Athens's conventions, and for this reason he is peculiarly estranged from his own land: deprived of a proper place—*atopos*, as he defines himself more than once.⁵ He is not *apolis* in the manner of the sophist, a stateless person deprived of formative rootedness; the philosopher inhabits a *polis* and is part of it, is a citizen, *polites*, in the full-fledged sense of the term. Yet, he dwells in the city and belongs to it in a very strange way. He does not necessarily come from another country, city, or state; rather, he seems to come from another world. And it is in this sense that we must interpret Socrates when he affirms that the philosopher is similar to a god, because of his elusive character (as we read in the *Sophist*),⁶ and that he is god-sent.⁷ It is precisely on his strangeness and foreignness to the manners and rules of the *polis* that Socrates insists in his speech before the law: "And so, men of Athens, this I ask and beg of you: if you hear me defend myself with the same speeches I am used to doing in the streets, near the banks of the money-changers, where many of you have heard me, and elsewhere, do not be surprised and do not grumble. In fact, this is how things are: I am here in court for the first time, at seventy years of age, and therefore lacking in technique and a foreigner [*xenos*] to this way of speaking."⁸ A stranger to forensic practices as much as to the rhetorical techniques of the sophists, Socrates expresses his peculiar condition in terms of inadequacy: he inhabits the community in the mode of nonbelonging, participates in the life of the community while remaining extraneous to the juridico-institutional theater. Significant, in this sense, is the constant appeal to the "men of Athens" that punctuates Socrates's speech and gradually sets into focus the contrast between collective identity and the stranger, and above all between institutional

---

3. Friedrich Nietzsche, *Works*, vol. 19, ed. O. Crusius and W. Nestle (Leipzig: Alfred Kröner, 1913), 237–239.
4. Plato, *Crito* 50a–54e.
5. Plato, *Apology* 31c; *Phaedrus* 229c; also: *Sophist* 216c–d.
6. Plato, *Sophist* 216a–c.
7. Plato, *Apology* 30d–31a.
8. Plato, *Apology* 17c–d.

actors and the transgressor. By his own words, the philosopher seems to wander with greater ease in the open space of the marketplace, the place where the exchange of goods takes place, where the *polis* itself in its basic necessity takes place. Analogously to the first city imagined in the *Republic*,[9] here the marketplace reveals the elementary ground of the life of the *polis*: labor and exchange. Assimilable neither to the private sphere of the family, nor to the public space of juridico-political debate, the fundamental dimensions of need and of interdependence, both among individuals inside the same *polis* and among different cities, are made manifest in the market square. This dawning city does not yet know physicians, histrionic masters of *logos*, servants, artists—in short, the variegated multitude of figures of malaise and decadence.[10]

But this does not mean that the philosopher is culturally uprooted. On the contrary, one could say that he finds himself at odds with his own city precisely because he maintains a much more intimate and more vigilant contact with the past and the cultural background from which the city comes. What for the city has become tradition, and is therefore retained as simulacrum, for the philosopher becomes an occasion for a close and discerning (and therefore critical and creative) encounter. The relation with the Homeric-heroic tradition is an example of this. Notwithstanding Homer's absolute institutional prestige in the Greek world of the fifth century, it is in the confrontation with the philosopher that the Homeric legacy, besides being retained and celebrated, comes back to life, is profoundly—even polemically—interrogated. In this hand-to-hand encounter the song, the actions, the heroes are taken seriously. In other words, as surprising as it may sound, it is the philosopher, Socrates, who is Homer's true friend.[11]

Friendship of the Dead

In fact, in the encounter between the philosopher and the ancient poet, the latter is not merely eradicated, expelled, as we often hear it said with extraordinary casualness. No. The figures of the Homeric *epos* are retained and, in their richness and vitality, observed in their becoming, in their transformational potential.

A fundamental element of Socrates's self-defense in the tribunal is the rewriting of the epic repertoire (but then again the assimilation of the

---

9. Plato, *Republic* 369b–372d.
10. Plato, *Republic* 373a–373d.
11. Plato, *Republic* 595b–c.

warrior's *ethos* to the concerns of philosophy is present throughout the Platonic *corpus*). The retention of poetic material gives rise to a most original twist—even a transfiguration of the heroic profile and of its prerogatives. Socrates compares himself to Thetis's son, Achilles—to his contempt for danger and his intrepidness in the face of death:

> You are not speaking beautifully, man, if you think that someone of value should at all take into account the risk of living and dying. In his actions, he should rather look after this only: whether what he does is just or unjust, whether he is behaving as a good man would, or a bad one. According to your reasoning, those demi-gods and all the others who died before Troy would not be worthy of much attention, in particular the son of Thetis, who would not be preoccupied with risk, so as not to be ashamed. Indeed when his mother, a goddess, spoke to him, who ardently wished to kill Hector, more or less as follows: "Son, if you will avenge the death of your friend Patroclos and kill Hector, you will die as well, for immediately after Hector's death your own is to follow"—hearing this he ignored danger and death, fearing much more to live shamefully and not avenge his friends. And he said, "May I die at once after inflicting the just punishment to the unjust, instead of remaining here exposed to ridicule, by the curved ships, a burden to the earth." Do you perhaps think that he thought much of death and danger?[12]

The Homeric hero displays a surprising similarity with the philosopher. He, too, bears the essential marks of the reject: his incomparable beauty and bravery make him extraordinary among human beings, disagreeable to the gods, and excluded from the communities of both. In the alchemical vessel of this superimposition of the two figures, traditional virile values, the ideal of man and of masculinity, are radically altered. Courage is no longer an excellence to be displayed literally and exclusively on the battlefield, but in any life circumstance. It consists in steadfastness in the face of danger, in the capacity to endure, to "stay and run the risk, not caring about death or anything else."[13]

Even if only implicitly, such a reconfiguration of heroic intrepidity involves a profound critique of conventional crystallizations. Excellence in combat becomes the capacity to bear the philosophical *praxis*—that is, to live philosophically, even if doing so would amount to living the most

---

12. Plato, *Apology* 28b–d.
13. Plato, *Apology* 28d.

obscure of lives, and the least recognized: "If one who really fights for the just is to preserve even for a short time his safety, he must of necessity lead a private, not a public, life."[14] This statement is confirmed in the concluding myth of the *Republic*, where the choice of living a "private" life, far from the clamors of public exposure and of fame, comes to be framed as a sign of a maturity conquered through harsh circumstances. It is the soul that was once Odysseus that, toward the end of the myth, makes this choice, and declares that it no longer seeks honor in the acts of warfare, thus demonstrating its emancipation from the thirst for glory, and giving proof of a new freedom. No longer subjected to the rules of approval and applause, freed from the anxiety of appearance, this soul lives through a reorientation that inaugurates the search for what is just, even in the shadow, even in invisibility.[15]

So, this transfigured hero that the philosopher is, endures all kinds of adversity to follow his path (his passion, necessity, the voice within). Analogously to the figure of Antigone, his position relative to the community shows that forms of authority and of political power, on the one hand, and justice, on the other, are not the same thing. Socrates recalls having opposed both the democratic regime and that of the Thirty Tyrants, in order not to be part of actions that he considered "outside the law,"[16] "unjust," or impious:[17] "And while there were orators ready to prosecute me and take me before the judges, and you were shouting and inciting them, I thought I should run any and every risk siding with law and justice rather than with you and unjust deliberations, for fear of prison or death."[18] Socrates therefore fights for the laws and with the laws (*nomoi*), as an expression of an infinite tension toward justice and not as an instrument of power's arbitrariness. For it is not by the laws, but by human beings, that Socrates suffers injustice.[19]

To the "men of Athens," then, Socrates seems to say, I am not one of you. This is how Hegel caught the force, at once disruptive and innovative, embodied in Socrates: "Socrates' principle manifests as a revolutionary moment against the Athenian state. . . . At that time, in Athens, that superior principle that signaled the destruction of the Athenian state's

---

14. Plato, *Apology* 32a.
15. Plato, *Republic* 620c–d.
16. Plato, *Apology* 32b.
17. Plato, *Apology* 32d.
18. Plato, *Apology* 32b–c.
19. Plato, *Crito* 54b–c.

substantial hold, advanced ever more in its development." The "revolutionary" character of Socratic reflection manifests itself in the figure of the *daimonion*: in being in a threshold position, intermediate, never completely out of this world, in tireless movement. And Socrates exhibits the unheard-of impact, the estranging and destabilizing power of the *daimonion*, threatening to overwhelm "reality" as it has come to be configured in the world that surrounds him.[20] His gaze is lucidly analytical, does not play according to the rules, and frees up the possibility of new moves and directions. But Socrates shows no sign of an inclination to stabilize, to let possible new arrangements emerge and be fixed in a definitive form. This role will be up to others, at a later time. In the figure of Socrates, philosophy is a mode of research with unhinging effects; it interrupts, brings about restlessness; it persists in the nascent (precisely revolutionary) state, without overly caring for the work of instituting. It is critique in its pure state. But this means that Socrates remains at inaccessible heights, defenseless, deprived of protective worldly structures. He dwells in the greatest risk.

Men and Women

It is perhaps in this spirit that an extraordinary passage, toward the end of the *Apology*, should be read. At this point, Socrates is turning to those who have supported him before the judges as well as before the trial, voting for his acquittal, and, above all, having shared with him a life of inquiry, of consciousness and self-consciousness: "I would like to discuss what has happened with those who voted for my acquittal, while the officers of the court are busy and I am not yet going there where I must die. So, men, stay with me for now: nothing prevents us from telling stories to each other until it is allowed. To you, for you are friends, I want to show the meaning of what has happened today. For, judges—calling you judges I believe I am calling you correctly—something wondrous has happened to me."[21] With such "judges" Socrates speaks of what, as far as he can tell, death might be. With these words, pronounced toward the end of his discourse, "Socrates's principle" seems to fill the abyssal discontinuity between life and death, between the place of mortals and the absence of place (or the altogether other topology) of the immortals.

---

20. G. W. F. Hegel, *Vorlesungen über die Philosophie der Geschichte* (Leipzig: Reclam, 1924), 350.

21. Plato, *Apology* 39e–40a.

In the manner of Er, the *angelos*-warrior of the *Republic*, or of Eros, the *daimon* evoked in the *Symposium*, such a "principle" remains operative through the unspeakable passage "to another place."[22]

> If, on the other hand, death is a migration from here to another place, and if what they say is true, namely, that all those who died are there, what greater good can there be than this, judges? For if anyone, arrived in Hades and freed from the so-called judges here, will find those who truly are judges, who, so they say, sit in judgement there, Minos and Rhadamanthus, and Aeacus, and Triptolemus and the other demi-gods who were just in their life, would this be a negligible transition? Again, what would each one of you give to be with Orpheus and Musaeus, and Hesiod, and Homer? If these things are true, I am ready to die many times. Especially for me, it would be wonderful to spend time there: if I were to meet Palamedes and Ajax, son of Telamon, and any other of the ancients who died because of an unjust sentence, I would compare my experience with theirs. I don't think it would be unpleasant.[23]

With these words, Socrates defuses the automatism that associates death with fear. Precisely because it is beyond the reach of illumination and comprehension, precisely because it is unknowable in the most definitive sense, death cannot, strictly speaking, be feared. If anything, it is fear that becomes noteworthy, that shows itself worthy of being interrogated. But death, in its impenetrability, can only provide the occasion for an imaginative exercise, for an attempt to expand the experience of this life, pushing it beyond itself: "And to be sure, most remarkably, I could spend time examining and interrogating people there, just as I do with those here, to understand who among them is wise and who thinks he is, but is not. What would each one of you give, judges, in order to examine the one who led the great army against Troy, or Odysseus, or Sisyphus, or the many other men and women one could mention?"[24] The visionary and transgressive dimension of the Socratic challenge appears here in full evidence. There is no reason to fear the unknown, and hence, no reason to fear death. Precisely because it is incomprehensible, death should not—and, in fact, cannot—be a cause for any anxiety, but should rather inspire contemplation of its extraordinary possibilities. Thus, in death Socrates comes to imagine another life, another place in which he could share

---

22. Plato, *Apology* 40e.
23. Plato, *Apology* 40e–41b.
24. Plato, *Apology* 41b–c.

his passion for inquiry and self-examination with ancient generations of judges, just ones, poets, and heroes—a place where he could hear their challenges in their own voices and compare them with his own experience. As in Athens, there Socrates could delight in the company of those around him, their lives, their stories. There, he would engage them all: "men and women," he now cares to specify, no longer being forced to address only the "men of Athens." Throughout his discourse, he referred to the "men of Athens" with sober precision, since women were not admitted into the courtroom, as in public spaces generally. Now, the hearing concluded and verdict returned, Socrates is free from the constrictions of "reality"—that is, from the configuration of the real in his own time, in the context of his own hometown. Now he can imagine places where it is possible to address himself not only to Athenians, nor only to men. He can imagine otherwise and speak accordingly.

At this point, his accusers, inadequate to the task of discerning and judging, are left behind. The physical scene of the courtroom, in its exclusively masculine public dimensions, seems to have been transcended. Now Socrates speaks as if he were alone with the few friends and "authentic judges" present in the transfigured courtroom, and he shares with them the fantastic vision of a world in which "men and women" live together under the sign of thinking, share their vicissitudes, confront the task of understanding themselves, one through the others, but also put each other to the test, "give each other a hard time," "limit" one another—spurring and inspiring each other as friends do.[25] For friendship is no complacency. It is with this delightful hypothesis, with the projection of such a world, that Socrates's discourse in self-defense draws to a close. Having evoked the company of those who are no longer, Socrates adds, "To converse and stay with them, and examine them, would be inconceivable happiness. At any rate, the people there do not kill for it."[26]

The adjective here translated as "immeasurable" is, in the Greek, *amechanon*, a word that amplifies the recurrence of the adverb *atechnos*, which appears several times in the text. Socrates seems to indicate a dimension that is nontechnical, noncontrived, nonstrategic, and, in the final analysis, exceeding his investigation and passion. The happiness here in play is inconceivable in the sense that it cannot be a matter of

---

25. Plato, *Apology* 41e. See *Meno* 81a, *Phaedrus* 235b. See, too, Peter Kingsley, *Ancient Philosophy, Mystery, and Magic: Empedocles and Pythagorean Tradition* (Oxford: Clarendon, 1995), 149–171.

26. Plato, *Apology* 41c.

ideation or devising. No technical mastery, machination, stratagem, or any other resource of the calculating intellect relates to it or can procure it. A certain lack of resources or, at the limit, a certain impotence, seem to distinguish the philosopher from the epic hero, characterized in Homer as astute and shrewd (paradigmatically, Odysseus is called *polymechanos*, "of much shrewedness," starting from *Iliad* II.173). The philosopher distinguishes themselves by doing what they can, not what they want.

Taken by an indominable vision of happiness, the philosopher glimpses a possibility, divines a reverberation of what the human can do and be. Such an experience of rapture (overwhelming, potentially devastating to human constructions) acts as an inexorable reminder of the irreducibility of humans to their own institutions. Reminds the human being of what, in them, surpasses the human dimension, indicating what they can become. The philosopher reveals the human precisely in the thrust beyond themselves, in that availability to the possible and within the possible. In philosophical experience, the human being to come is at once recalled and announced.

Thus, in the philosophical inflection the hero becomes something radically other: an inaugural figure, who retains the traces of a legacy but also allows for a new humanity to be presaged; a disarmed warrior, without name and reputation, for whom fighting and combat happen far from the battlefield, from competitions, from honors and prizes. But this transfiguring work on epic material entails still further suggestions. The Socratic vision of another world, one in which "men and women" can confront one another and grow together, conjures up a community of friends as a community of dialogue and inquiry. It is noteworthy that Socrates explicitly includes women, here. In Plato and in the Pythagorean tradition, this gesture is frequent and, at the same time, in sharp contrast to the customs of the *polis*. And, we should say, not only in contrast with fifth- and fourth-century Athens, if it is true that before long the philosophical discourse itself will end up celebrating friendship as an exclusive relation between men.

This framing of friendship will prove extremely long-lived. Montaigne will still say that, "to tell the truth, the ordinary capacity of women is inadequate for that communion and fellowship which is the nurse of this sacred bond; nor does their soul seem firm enough to endure the strain of so tight and durable a knot."[27] The obstacle to a friendship

---

27. Michel de Montaigne, "Of Friendship," in *The Complete Essays of Montaigne*, trans. D. M. Frame (Stanford, CA: Stanford University Press, 1966), 138.

extended to women seems to be, again, the wildness and incontrollable power of physical passions. Nietzsche, too, will remark that woman is "as yet incapable of friendship," just like the slave (who cannot "be a friend") and the tyrant (who cannot "have friends"). Woman—cat, bird, or even cow—knows nothing but delirious love.[28] But, to remain with Montaigne, he completes his reflection on women and friendship in this way: "And indeed, but for that, if such a relationship, free and voluntary, could be built up, in which not only would the souls have this complete enjoyment, but the bodies would also share in the alliance, so that the entire man would be engaged, it is certain that the resulting friendship would be fuller and more complete. But this sex in no instance has yet succeeded in attaining it, and by the common agreement of the ancient schools is excluded from it."[29] Perhaps Montaigne had second thoughts on this point, as it appears in the posthumously published essay "Of Presumption," where a mixture of love and admiration for the young Marie de Gournay leads him to predict that she could "some day" be capable of the most complete friendship.[30] However, for long stretches of Western cultural history, such affirmations are rare, partial, or absent. One of the most notable documents in this fragile thread is *The Subjection of Women*, by J. S. Mill (1869), even though the author limits himself to considering friendship between woman and man. And Virginia Woolf's invitation to concede that women do not always detest one another, feel jealous of each other, or catfight over men, sounds bitterly mocking: "Do not start. Do not blush. Let us admit it in the privacy of our own society that these things sometimes happen. Sometimes women do like women."[31]

To sustain the thesis of feminine inadequacy in matters of friendship, Montaigne appeals to the authority of the ancients. Nevertheless, the Platonic Socrates seems to tell another story. Of course, as we said before, Socrates was no scholarch, no man of institution. And his story is so unusual, so daringly far from the narratives already dominant in his time, as to be nearly inaudible. But, as evanescent as Socrates's appeal

---

28. Friedrich Nietzsche, "On the Friend," *Thus Spoke Zarathustra*, Part I.
29. Montaigne, "Of Friendship," 138.
30. *The Complete Essays of Montaigne*, trans. D. M. Frame (Stanford, CA: Stanford University Press, 1966), 502. On the posthumous edition of the essays, edited by M. de Gournay, see Kuisma Korhonen, *Textual Friendship: The Essay as Impossible Encounter from Plato and Montaigne to Levinas and Derrida* (Amherst, NY: Prometheus Books, 2006), 279–285.
31. Virginia Woolf, *A Room of One's Own* (London: Hogarth Press, 1929), chapter 5.

to the community of men and women may be, its ubiquity in Platonic thought must surely be recognized. Here, too, let us limit ourselves to a single example—the most minute and punctiform, but far from negligible: the story of Alcestis, "she who is strong."

"Moved Life"

This time, it is Phaedrus who narrates, and the context is the *Symposium*. The passage, however short, is so saturated with revelatory details that it is worth citing in its entirety:

> Only those who love are ready to die for the beloved, not only men, but women too. Alcestis, the daughter of Pelias, is for the Greeks sufficient proof for this assertion, being the only one willing to die for her husband, even though he still had a father and a mother. In virtue of her love [*eros*], she greatly surpassed them in friendship [*philia*], demonstrating that they were like strangers to their son, parents only in name. After she actually carried out this action, it seemed to the gods as well as human beings so beautifully performed, and the gods so admired it, that they allowed her soul to come back (although many others have performed many beautiful actions, but seldom have the gods granted such a gift, sending the soul back from Hades). To such an extent do the gods themselves honor in particular the dedication and excellence coming from love.[32]

Love changes the connection with life, and so with death. Whoever loves finds themselves free before death. The name of this attitude is "courage," *andreia*, the masculine virtue *par excellence*. Phaedrus had mentioned it a little earlier, underlining precisely how its lack (*anandreia*) is the deplorable and sure sign of a nature of little value.[33] Hence, Alcestis is the woman who has courage: capable of dying—that is, of facing fear—for Admetus, her beloved.[34] Compared to her, it is Admetus, rather, who shows himself to be lacking in courage, unresolved, overwhelmed by her strength. Admetus had obtained Alcestis's hand by demonstrating that he could subjugate two wild beasts, a boar and a lion, and bend them to the yoke;[35] but now he appears fearful, eager to take advantage, by any

---

32. Plato, *Symposium* 179b–d.
33. Plato, *Symposium* 178d.
34. On the courage of women, see Plutarch, *Gynaikon aretai*, as well as lyric authors like Telesilla of Argos and Corinna of Tanagra.
35. Pseudo-Apollodorus, *Library* I.9.15; Hygini, *Fabulae* 50.

means available, of Apollo's favor, who would grant him a prolongation of life, on condition that someone take his place in Hades. And yet Alcestis, she who possesses the excellence of men, is not thereby a man. She is the woman who draws anew the meaning of intimacy in contrast to extraneity, of true familiarity in contrast to the convention of family names. She is the one who can offer herself in the most extreme, excessive act, outside the established customs of measure and the moderation of the conformists. Just like the true lovers Socrates speaks of elsewhere, whose freedom, profundity, and intensity of feeling make them completely unassimilable to the rules grounding the juridico-political edifice.[36] Like Alcestis, such lovers share very little of the conventional male profile.

It has been said that Alcestis embodies the archetypal feminine desire of self-sacrifice for her man.[37] But it is more probable that she is simply a figure of the hyperbolic experience inscribed in the depth of affection, of every affect as such: the woman who lives the union of *eros* and *philia*, and who understands that love is devotion, donation, recognizing that one belongs to an other and does own oneself, that one is not only for the other but of the other. In the end, Platonic language—most subtle, as always—leaving behind the man-woman duality, says that, together with the gods, it is not men but "human beings" (*anthropoi*) who note Alcestis with admiration.

Alcestis's episode brings fresh air to the reflection on friendship, on the tonality intrinsic to the constitution of community, of plurality, of each of us in light of the "we" and as "we." And it does not matter if this pronoun, "we" (but no less the other pronoun, "I"), is, ultimately, unpronounceable, because of the heterogeneous multiplicity gathered in it. Friendship is a place of paradoxes and, ultimately, of enigmatically shifting pronouns. Even in its constancy and steadfastness, it is *hyperbole*, excess, and overturns even the most balanced discourse devoted to measure, equilibrium, and commensurability—that is, to convenience. Friendship is "the moved life" (*das bewegte Leben*), to cite Aby Warburg, who, with this expression, intended to encompass the very essence of ancient thought.[38] Life moving, and therefore moved, as in a photo

---

36. Plato, *Phaedrus* 256e–257a.
37. Alberto Savinio, *Alcesti di Samuele* (Milan: Bompiani, 1949); also Gavino Piga, *L'Alcesti di Euripide nell'Alcesti secondo Alberto Savinio* (Torino: Accademia University Press, 2016).
38. Aby Warburg, *Werke in einem Band*, ed. M. Treml, S. Weigel, and P. Ladwig (Berlin: Suhrkamp, 2010), 63.

shooting, as in the wind-filled veils of a nymph: the originary *pathos* of a humanity that, far from standing out in sharp, sculptural, hyper-rational, and sovereignly austere relief, barely delineates itself while it already undoes itself in what surrounds it—its trembling borders, caught in desire, impetuous, indefinite, changing.

5. PHILOSOPHERS' FRIENDSHIP

Teachers and Students

Earlier we mentioned the "friends of ideas." Friendship for the ideas, for a certain type of contemplation and existential posture, transcends each of the friends individually and unites them all, such that they are also and crucially friends among themselves. This is the philosophers' friendship, where the act of *philein* signals a predilection, a dual belonging: one belongs affectively both to common inquiry and to those who share it with us. But what does this mean? A friendship with such immense consequences that it almost disappears in its concreteness—that between Plato and Aristotle—can tell us something about this. Their twenty-year companionship is well worth a very brief digression.

There is a point in the *Nicomachean Ethics* that reveals the philosophers' *modus operandi*. Speaking here is probably the mature Aristotle who, reflecting on the good, differentiates himself from those who meditated on this same topic and develops a critical evaluation of their results. Aristotle does not name Plato explicitly. He limits himself to mentioning the "friends," plural, who speak of the "ideas"—presumably Platonists such as Speusippus and Xenocrates. It is precisely by fine-tuning his critical analysis of the Platonists' doctrines that Aristotle comes to bring into focus his own perspective on the good. And this, in itself, is already noteworthy: the comparison, the specification of differences, even of discordances, prove to be essentially generative. In this confrontation the positions, or even just the hypotheses, can be articulated with greater incisiveness, in view of a progressive maturation.

And yet, "such an inquiry is inaugurated with great reluctance," Aristotle informs us, since the men (*andras*) "who introduced the ideas are friends." Yet, he continues, "one should perhaps consider it better, and also a matter of duty, to forsake even what is close so as to save the truth, especially because we are philosophers; for while both [friends and truth] are dear to us, it is pious to honor the truth."[1] It would seem that Aristotle is opposing the love of "truth" to the love of friends, giving priority to the former to the exclusion of the latter. But, on closer inspection, a much more complex play of mirrors and references is revealed here. Without saying so, Aristotle is in fact quoting his mentor, who expresses himself in an analogous way precisely in his "esoteric"—that is, public—writings. In Book X of the *Republic*, Plato has Socrates say that, even in reaffirming his friendship and admiration for Homer, he will pursue the truth above all.[2] In the *Phaedo*, again, Socrates urges his friends to worry not about Socrates, but rather about the truth.[3] Plato attributes this posture toward the friend to Socrates himself, both when at stake is Socrates's attitude toward friends (for example, Homer) and when the issue is the attitude of other friends (for example, Simmias and Cebes) toward Socrates. This casts light on the connection between the reciprocity of friendship and self-reflexivity: between the experience of being reciprocated and the capacity of placing oneself in the role of the other. The relation of friendship—and, in particular, the friendship that lies at the heart of the philosophical posture—displays an inevitable element of passivity, of receptivity, intertwined with action. In friendship, in love, in philosophy, transcendence is evidenced. The increasing awareness that being together always involves transcending and being transcended illuminates a play of exceedances, cross-references, amplifications, and ulteriority, in which the friend's finitude, far from being diminished, comes to light up in its beauty and potentiality.

Hence, Aristotle cites Plato; Plato, in turn, cites Socrates (or in any case, in his theatrical game of attributions, traces his words back to Socrates). Each cites their own teacher who, at least if the citation is

---

1. Aristotle, *Nicomachean Ethics* 1096a12–16.
2. Plato, *Republic* 595b–c.
3. Plato, *Phaedo* 91b–c.

to be trusted, says, Friend, do not so much mind me, but pursue your own inquiry. Truth: this we love and seek together. So, setting aside one's teacher—or, in any case, subjecting them to critique—does not mean rejecting them, but rather repeating their free gesture, taking up that freedom that is identical to responsibility, becoming, in turn, oneself a teacher, a teacher and student at once. In this gesture lies the availability to contemplate one's own limit along with the limit of the teacher. Aristotle's comment contains a sublime form of fidelity, according to which the student is inscribed within a lineage of teachings freely imparted and received, in a common research open beyond each one, which from Plato goes back to Socrates, from Socrates to the archaic poet, until it dissolves in the boundlessness and anonymity of the most remote past. Distancing himself from Plato, Aristotle testifies to his greatness and honors him, demonstrating that friendship is neither imitative mirroring, nor deference, but mutual inspiration. Even friendship with one's teacher.

Resonances

Therefore, the statement that seems to oppose friendship to truth, and to establish the latter's privilege, is in fact possible thanks to the reference to the friend. The quotation of the friend stands as condition and foundation of truth's privilege, becoming inconspicuous almost to the point of disappearing, in such a way as to leave only the truth in relief. This, however, does not escape Thomas Aquinas, who reveals the friends' actual closeness concealed in the apparent tension between friendship and love of the true. In his commentary on the *Nicomachean Ethics*, displaying his usual equanimity, he observes, "Along the same lines is also the judgment of Plato who, in rejecting the opinion of his teacher Socrates, says a man ought to care more for truth than anything else. Somewhere else he affirms that Socrates is certainly his friend, however, truth is still more so [*amicus quidem Socrates sed magis amica veritas*]. And in yet another place he says that we should care a little for Socrates but a great deal for the truth."[4] Roger Bacon, too, underlines how concordant Aristotle's gesture is with Plato[5]—citing as sources, besides the *Nicomachean Ethics*, the pseudo-Aristotelian treatise *Secretum Secretorum* (translated from Arabic into Latin between the twelfth and thirteenth century), as well as

---

4. Thomas Aquinas, *Sententia libri Ethicorum* I.6.5.
5. Roger Bacon, *Opus Majus* I.v.

Life of Aristotle, often attributed to Ammonius Hermiae but of uncertain origin.[6]

Thus, just as soon as the friendship between "men" is set aside (to favor the company of the truth), it is evoked anew, albeit transformed. Friendship between "men" is reaffirmed in the form of friendship between and among the friends of wisdom. For "we," says Aristotle with emphasis, "are philosophers." And philosophers are those exemplary friends who nurture the same passion for wisdom, even though the way in which each engages and conducts their inquiry is unique, and may lead to contrasting results to those of others. The same thrust can be shared in many ways. This is well highlighted by friendship, and it is in virtue of this that friendship does not so much imply agreement—that is, saying the same things, formulating the same doctrines—but rather undergoing the same experience (*pathos*), being exposed to the same question, sharing a certain relation with truth that entails its continuous questioning. At the center of friendship, then, is a certain comportment in relation to truth, which is studied, loved, but neither possessed, nor known, much less mastered. So understood, friendship and passion for the truth are neither mutually excluding alternatives, nor incompatible: friendship rests on the shared love of truth, and this love finds in friendship the favorable condition for unfolding itself in investigation, experience, contemplation.

And yet, if, on the one hand, desire joins, on the other it demands an inexorable exploration, prompts each to trace their own path of investigation— that is to say, it does not lead to acquiescence toward friends and teachers. From a common impulse, see the unfolding of trajectories that are in tension with one another, when not in altogether open conflict. The philosopher's *ethos* is motivated by a love for the truth that does not remain trapped in dogmatic alliances, in forms of fidelity that demand the suspension of investigation. Thus, pursuing wisdom together, as friends, will not have entailed arriving at the same results, but rather cultivating together a certain bearing, a life dedicated to studying the things of the

---

6. Henry Guerlac notes that the saying in question appears with variations in *Life of Aristotle*, which is found in three distinct medieval manuscripts, two in Greek and one in Latin: Henry Guerlac, "*Amicus Plato* and Other Friends," *Journal of the History of Ideas* 39, no. 4 (1978): 627–633. See also Leonardo Tarán, "*Amicus Plato, sed magis amica veritas*: From Plato and Aristotle to Cervantes," *Antike und Abendland* 30 (1984): 93–124; repr. in *Collected Papers (1962–1999)* (Leiden: Brill, 2001), 3–46.

world, and above all oneself. The friendship between philosophers, then, makes particularly clear what concerns friendship as such. The friend says, Friend, precisely in making sure that your friendship for me does not foreclose your horizons, you will be my friend; consider me an occasion for openness, an invitation to not confine yourself; and may fidelity not come to signify stiffening and arbitrary limitation.

In philosophical love just as in the love for an other, what is at stake is the sharing of what exceeds the bond between two or more human beings. In this sense, there is no contention between philosophy and friendship, since both are animated by the love of what cannot be reduced to the two (or more) friends and what can go by many names. Friends find, in one another, a reminder of what is irreducible to one just as to the other. They love each other precisely because each sees in the other the same overflowing love that never imprisons the other in an exiguous, asphyxiating, or exclusionary bond. Just as Aristotle shows in the relationship with friends, and above all in his relationship with Plato, intimacy with the friend is the place where one learns distance, a diverging that is not a conflict but ampler belonging. Maurice Blanchot writes, "What separates: what puts authentically in relation, the very abyss of relations in which lies, with simplicity, the agreement of friendly affirmation that is always maintained."[7]

And, in any case, it would remain to be seen if the good according to Aristotle would actually be wholly other than that of Platonic thought. A certain Platonism formulates the good in its abstract universality, as an intelligible principle that inflects itself in infinite sensible manifestations. Aristotle, as we well know, distances himself from this. Certainly, he focuses on the good as that toward which all human activity seems to tend,[8] the knowledge of which is of the greatest value precisely as the orientation of our living and acting.[9] And his inquiry is no less ambitious than the Platonic one, for it is within the horizon of the good, in the most comprehensive sense, that human ventures and assessments are situated. But his thinking rejects any conceptual or mathematical reduction of the good, in polemical opposition to those who "on the basis of numbers demonstrate that justice and health are a good . . . on the assumption that the good lies in numbers and monads, for the good itself

---

7. Maurice Blanchot, *Friendship*, trans. Elizabeth Rottenberg (Stanford, CA: Stanford University Press, 1997), 292.
8. Aristotle, *Nicomachean Ethics* 1094a1–5.
9. Aristotle, *Nicomachean Ethics* 1094a19–28.

is the one."[10] Hence, he posits the good (the fact "that" there is such a thing on which we confer this name), without being able to establish demonstratively (scientifically) "what" it may be. Just like being, the good can be said "in many ways" and, consequently, cannot be comprised unproblematically within one science.[11] Indeed, Aristotle does not avoid the question concerning "what" the good may be;[12] however, he warns that "what excellence or the good is in life escapes our investigation."[13]

But, to be precise, Plato says exactly the same thing in the *Philebus*. The old teacher reemerges in his student's reflections. Or perhaps, through many years of frequentation and shared practice, the teacher himself has become a student as well, and the student a teacher. The fact is that at the end of this late dialogue, Plato has Socrates, who was trying to get close to the good in order to grasp its essence, say, "Now the power of the good has fled for us into the nature of the beautiful."[14] The flight of the good into the beautiful entails an obscuring of the first in the splendor of the second. It marks an inaccessibility: the good as such may be intuited in the beautiful but, at the same time, it becomes unapproachable, precisely to the extent to which it appears. For the good is not of the order of visibility, and is therefore, at the same time, preserved in beauty and betrayed by it. It hides there, in magnificent splendor, despite (or precisely in virtue of) being in itself radically other than any place and splendor.

The presumed doctrinal contrast between Plato and Aristotle, concerning the good, would deserve a finer assessment, even beyond this dialogue. To be sure, Plato employs the formula "the idea of the good," thereby placing the good on the ontological level (ideas are, in fact, articulations of being, they express the "what" of what is). We find this expression in *Republic* VI,[15] and yet it is immediately called into question; in the development of the same argument the good is characterized as "beyond being"—that is, beyond the order of ideas.[16] This is also reaffirmed in the celebrated analogy of the sun and of the good, at once disarming and decisive: just as the sun is the source of light that reveals visible things to

---

10. Aristotle, *Nicomachean Ethics* 1218a18–21.
11. Aristotle, *Nicomachean Ethics* 1096a24–34; *Eudemian Ethics* 1217b27–1218a1.
12. Aristotle, *Eudemian Ethics* 1217b1.
13. Aristotle, *Eudemian Ethics* 1216a9–10.
14. Plato, *Philebus* 64e.
15. Plato, *Republic* 508c–509a.
16. Plato, *Republic* 509b.

sight, so the good is the source of "the being and truth" that illuminate intelligible things, revealing them to intellectual perception.[17] Therefore the good, far from being an idea among ideas, emerges as a condition of the possibility of ideas: as what makes ideas possible, bringing them to light, luminous and perceptible, and therefore making possible their perception by the intellect. The good would be the source and root of the intelligible order, the sphere in which the intelligibles and the intelligence that perceives them are given in their interdependence (just as, in the visible order, the visible and what sees it are given together). As the source of all knowledge, of knowability itself, it presents itself as radically unknowable.

Plato's path (*hodos*) is not the same as Aristotle's. In their singularities, paths never overlap, especially those of friends, it seems. And yet, the outcome Plato reaches—namely, the good in its unfathomable exorbitance, or even the fleeing and fugitive good—does not seem so distant from the conclusions reached by Aristotle, who indicates the insurmountable displacement of the good with respect to our attempts at definition and capture.

---

17. Plato, *Republic* 508d.

6. ON ENMITY

Via Negativa

For both Aristotle and his teacher, the vicissitudes of friendship and those of justice present themselves as intimately connected. The *Republic* brings this vividly to light: the dialogue that pursues an understanding of justice (this, too, as fleeting as the good)[1] unfolds in its entirety as a long meditation on friendship, on a bond of solidarity at first limited to our own, our kin, those partaking in the narrow context of our immediate surroundings, and then on the possibility of widening gradually the circle that we trace around ourselves, and thus our capacity, our spaciousness, and our sense of belonging to the world.

But, above all, the thinking here is turned to the disasters of friendship in its exclusionary version, which divides the world rather than uniting it, contracts the world rather than dilating it, identifies its own and, in one and the same gesture, the foreigner and the enemy. In many ways, then, at stake is a *via negativa* toward friendship. We approach friendship in moving through its absence, in traversing what it is not. We may recall that the *Republic* lingers at length on tyranny, the most infamous political constitution and (in virtue of the *psyche-polis* isomorphism) the most infernal psychical constitution. It is the most disharmonious setting,

---

1. Plato, *Republic* 432b–c.

both outside and inside: devastated by desires that have downgraded to rapacious impulses, a hostage to joyless cravings and bottomless appetites, corroded by doubts and dread. Here, ingenuity works to foment fear and close minds, creativity excogitates the proliferation of conflict, the production of enmity becomes an industry. These are pages, especially in *Republic* VIII and IX, of disturbing modernity. Or, perhaps, what is disturbing is a certain invariability. We, too, know well how easily ill will and discontent can be manipulated, how names are promoted and careers made thanks to the designation (that is, the invention) of an enemy, to the unscrupulous employment of conflict, to the engineering of fear. On the subject of the relation between friendship and justice, then, let us follow this other story that Plato narrates in the nocturnal dialogue. As by now we are intuiting, the stories it contains are many.

The Psycho-Political Scene

The dramatic date is probably around 411 BC, toward the end of the Peloponnesian War (which will see Athens defeated by Sparta) and on the eve of the Thirty Tyrants' oligarchy (which will trigger fatal events for many of the participants in the dialogue—Socrates included). When Plato is writing, all of them are dead, and it is in thinking with the dead that he tries to understand the problems that concern us here. The action unfolds at the Piraeus. Socrates went down to the port of Athens with Glaucon ("the shining one") to "see" (again, the posture of *theoria*) the festivities dedicated for the first time to a goddess unnamed in the dialogue, with processions organized both by the local population and by the people of Thrace. Socrates is preparing to return when he is intercepted by a group of friends who insist that he should remain and spend the evening with them. Socrates protests, tries to convince them to let him go. But, replies Polemarchus ("the lord of war"), what if we do not listen? "Could you seriously persuade us, if we won't listen?"[2] Despite the friendly tenor of the exchange, this is already the scene of a detention. Socrates, who would like to take the upward way and return to the city, is held down there and will have to break through, try to be heard, if he wants to earn his way back.

But meanwhile, he will be the one having to listen, and only thanks to this capacity shall he be able to speak efficaciously. He will have to be touched, expose himself, and thanks to this he may possibly touch in turn. Thus opens what will be an all-night dialogue.

---

2. Plato, *Republic* 327c.

Socrates is held back at the Piraeus, and from here on the strains and struggles multiply. In Polemarchus's house, the conversation moves to the topic of justice. Having argued that justice is giving what is appropriate to friends and enemies—that is, benefits to the former and harms to the latter—the young man is interrogated by Socrates. Eventually, they agree that "it is never just to harm someone," be they friend or enemy. But Thrasymachus ("the rash fighter"), one of the guests, refuses to be so easily convinced and attacks Socrates, stating that everyone knows how things really are: justice is the advantage of the stronger, of those who succeed in imposing themselves and prevailing over others, promoting their own exclusive advantage. Socrates discusses and dismantles the argument but, among those present, Glaucon and Adeimantus are unsatisfied with his argument: Socrates's position is unusual, it arouses a desire and a new yearning in them, so they want Socrates to speak about it further. To spur him, they both tell him that the position defended by Thrasymachus, in his defiant and provocative attitude, is in fact widely shared throughout the *polis*, albeit often discretely concealed. In a very lucid analysis that anticipates Hobbes's anthropological perspective (but also Nietzsche's, Freud's, and beyond), Glaucon reports what follows:

> They say that acting unjustly is by nature a good thing, while suffering injustice is bad; but that the badness in suffering injustice greatly exceeds the good in perpetrating it; so that, when committing and suffering injustice, and hence experiencing both, those who can neither avoid the latter nor choose the former hold it advantageous to establish an agreement among themselves, in order to exclude both doing and suffering injustice. From here, they began to institute their laws and covenants, and to call just and legal what the law prescribes. Such, then, seems to be the origin and being of justice; it lies between what is best (committing injustice without undergoing punishment) and what is worst (undergoing injustice without possibly taking revenge). The just is in the middle between these extremes, and held in high esteem, not because it is good, but because of the weakness in doing injustice. A true man capable of injustice would never establish such an agreement excluding unjust acts in order not to suffer injustice. He would be mad. Now, justice is of such kind, Socrates, and it naturally grows out of such things. So they say.[3]

---

3. Plato, *Republic* 358e–359b.

Community is possible to the extent that everyone agrees to the containment of their abusive and feral impulses. Justice would be such an accord or consensus: a contract. Staying together, then, would mean bearing one another, tolerating the limitation imposed on what each individual would do for their own interest, if they could. In Plato there is neither ingenuousness, nor what could be called an innocence of the ancients compared to the moderns. He knows all too well that this disenchanted vision of human nature and of the violent origin of human consortium is upheld by many, and unconsciously harbored by many more upstream of every reflection. And those who, now as well as then, indiscriminately say of everyone else "they're all the same," and who settle in discouragement and bitterness with excessive ease, ready to view everyone else's actions as prompted by despicable (and therefore unspeakable) motivations—don't they subscribe precisely to the widespread opinion reported so effectively by Plato's Glaucon? It is precisely as a counterpoint to this initial scenario that Socrates will imagine a *polis* of altogether different origins, and thus an altogether different humanity.

Already in Book II the conversation focuses on the *polis* as the accessible image of the *psyche*. From here on, this will be the *polis*: a more legible script, written in "larger letters," of the *psyche*, which in itself remains infinitely remote.[4] Nothing could be said of the *psyche* without reference to the *polis* and without presupposing their structural analogy. Politics and psychology are presented in their equiprimordiality—one as the writing of the other, and the other in turn as the invisible formula and motive of the one. To better grasp the structures of the *polis*, Socrates and the others consider how it originated, and we should notice right away that enmity plays no part in this origin; hostility, violence, war are not inscribed *ab origine* in the emergence of human community. This is a matter of great import and consequence: the fact that war may not be contemplated in the first articulation of the *polis* should be read as a Socratic response to the opinions voiced by Glaucon.

And thus we follow Socrates's narrative: a myth of origins (it must be a myth, for there is no science of origins)[5] through which transpires the solidarity sustaining both life inside the *polis* and its exchanges with other communities.[6] The "social contract" thesis expressed by Glaucon

---

4. Plato, *Republic* 368c–369a.
5. Plato, *Republic* 382d.
6. Plato, *Republic* 369b, 370e–371a.

presupposes monadically separate, autonomous individuals, in conflict with one another, and aims to overcome such natural violence by elevating it to state monopoly. To this thesis, Socrates replies by evoking a structural interdependence: each human being, just like each political body, lacks self-sufficiency, so great is its need of others. This is the cause, the reason why human beings gather together into a community, and communities communicate among themselves.

A Vision of Peace

This moment of the dialogue, thus, signals a decisive struggle. At stake is the definition of the originary impulse by which human community is stirred—hence, the definition of the human being in its being. Is the life that presents itself in human form ultimately and essentially destructive, or how might it be otherwise comprehended? As we shall see, war and destructiveness will enter the scene shortly thereafter—yet it is significant that the Socratic discourse admits them with a certain delay. However exiguous, such a delay is sufficient to negate their essentiality and ineluctability: the phenomenon of war is revealed as somehow secondary with respect to the originary scene, and thus not absolutely inevitable. Such a gap indicates a margin as yet unexhausted, a possibility of imagining otherwise, beyond what so far has proved to be historically pervasive and triumphant. History as we know it, then, does not exhaust the possible—and the past of which it constantly reminds us must not be understood as a prescription, much less a prophecy, of an identical future. Our historical memory, which everywhere testifies to the inevitability of war, cannot automatically become a denial of other developments and perpetuation of the same.

It is precisely this automatism that Socrates, in contemplating a peaceful, friendly origin of human coexistence, does not want to concede. Socrates—who still knows firsthand the facts of war, the disarray of battlefields, the devastation of civil life—refuses to take this automatism for granted; he defends as far as he can the divergence between the apparent necessity of war and an origin not crucially marked by war: he tries to preserve this noncoincidence, to hold back the facile and unreflective assumption that, if there has always been war, so it will always be. In this way he holds open a space and time not encumbered by what is past and predictable, but radically unthought, yet to be imagined. History, in sum, has not come to an end, nor can it claim to have completely actualized the possibilities inscribed in the origin—the origin that marked the beginning but also lives on in us and, thus marking us, governs and guides our life.

The originary *polis*, then, is illuminated in its characteristic traits of peace, harmony, and health. And it is not a case of a primitive, prepolitical aggregation but of an organism endowed with full institutional awareness: there are concerns not only with subsistence and the necessary, but also with the relation between measure and excess, between the human and the divine. Here, moments of recreation are expected, the gods are celebrated with festivities and songs, the attempt is made to procreate in conformity with one's own resources, so as to avoid war and poverty.[7] Commentators and scholars too often ignore altogether this auroral image of the *polis*, to move on hastily to the construction of the second *polis* that will occupy Books III–V. Everywhere, in the innumerable readings of the *Republic* as a "treatise" of "political science," the *polis* that will follow this first one is seen as the one true beginning of the Socratic-Platonic political constitution.

It should be noted that the city of origin is not, strictly speaking, *the* first city, but rather *a* city originally comprehended in the primordial scene of humanity distributed in multiple communities. The salubrious and peaceful city is always already implicated in the life of other cities: the organization, the organicity of the political space is not explained in terms of a single, self-sufficient city closed in on itself.[8] Instead, the hypothesis entails the mutual implication of the communities as well as of the individuals: the emerging of the *polis* at once highlights a net of political relations in which each *polis* belongs. The political space is the open space of differing, in which various communities variously interact among themselves, putting into play their differences. So much for Carl Schmitt and his epigones, who willfully attributed a Platonic ancestry to the theory of war (the logic that identifies the other with the enemy) as the foundation of the political as such, of its dynamics and inner coherence.

It should equally be underscored that the just community thus sketched does not include the presence of the philosopher. This figure will appear only later, when it will be a matter of bringing measure and discernment back into a *polis* compromised by its own boundless appetites. The activity of a Socrates himself is therefore superfluous in a community that lives harmoniously and develops itself in accord with what surrounds it.

---

7. Plato, *Republic* 372a–c.
8. Plato, *Republic* 371d.

That precisely this, in Socrates's view, should be the human condition in its happy fulfillment, is a revealing fact. In a certain sense, Socrates's dedication to philosophical—that is, dialectical and dialogical—exercise is complete; his commitment to self-examination and examination of the other is paradigmatic. Yet, in another sense, here we see Socrates ready to leave, to abandon the places that need philosophy as therapy and orientation. We see Socrates gladly imagine a place and time in which philosophy may not be necessary, a life friendly to itself and to things, without further analysis. The primordial *polis* therefore announces the possibility of a life without philosophy, or rather of a life in which philosophy reaches into the deepest recesses of the living organism and becomes life. In Socrates, philosophy extends beyond, not aspiring to self-preservation, to its own exercise as an end in itself, but rather opening itself to its own self-overcoming.

The figure of Socrates lets both attitudes seep through: called into question, Socrates cannot but listen, he cannot withdraw from the requests for help that are addressed to him by a suffering world (let us not forget that, right at the beginning of Book II, the two brothers, Glaucon and Adeimantus, had implored him to speak in favor of justice so as to turn them away from the cynical and conventional discourses prevailing in the city). Nevertheless, if circumstances like those imagined in the healthy or healed *polis* were to be brought about, then Socrates could also relieve himself of the philosophical task. Just as in the beginning of the dialogue, were he not held back at the Piraeus, Socrates would gladly return "home."[9]

Philosophy's silence, its transcending itself into life, into a contemplation irreducible to logical as well as dialogical work, is a complex matter. I limit myself to recalling, as but one example, the culminating moment of Socrates's discourse in the *Symposium*, the platonic text on love.[10] At the high point of knowledge's ascent toward the beautiful, when at stake would be the perception of the beautiful itself, Socrates hints at an overcoming of discursive knowledge. He speaks of a contemplation without science (*episteme*) and without discourse (*logos*), of an *immediate* perception of what shines through the many beautiful phenomena, making them glow: an insight that may arrive when one still is in the company of others (it is not a solitary experience), but not involving the shared

---

9. Plato, *Republic* 327b.
10. Plato, *Symposium* 210e–212a.

dialectical effort. Such contemplation can be achieved in the company of those whom we love for their beauty, looking at them and delighting in their presence.

Here, as indeed in Letter VII, Plato says that enlightening intuition, perception no longer mediated by *logos*, happens (if and when it happens) thanks to being with others, "suddenly."[11] Contemplation, thus, does not entail a withdrawal from the world and from the community: those who are loved are not abandoned, but fully enjoyed, along with the visions of the beautiful evoked thereby. One lives fully. And this would then be an other way of being together: other than the ordinary tensions of living together, but also other with respect to the philosophical sharing in discourse and research. Outlined here, albeit intermittently and *in limine*, is an unheard-of way of being-with, a community that, transcending discourse—that is, traversing discourse without being concluded therein—manages to "bring to light" (it is a matter of birth) excellence, beauty in actions, in the way of life.

It is to this community that one could perhaps compare the primeval *polis* of the *Republic*, so as to further clarify its character. In different contexts and different voices, Plato points to a philosophical exercise irreducible to the primacy of reason and rationality: a philosophical exercise that, albeit completely devoted to analytical practice and critical examination, still exceeds itself, transforming itself into something other, into a quiet stillness at once luminous and active, visionary and ethically (politically) fecund.

And Yet, Enemies

But, in the scene at the Piraeus, Socrates must confront more peculiar resistances, compared to the *Symposium*, and, once again, must submit to the demands of the situation. Glaucon interrupts him, forcing him to contend with the reality surrounding them: the reality of Athens in those days and of the luxurious house itself in which they are hosted. But how can it be, Socrates, that the inhabitants of your city feast with barley bread and wine? Where are spices and delicacies, where the elegant seats on which to recline, where all the superfluities necessary by now? Glaucon marks in this way the transition from the *polis* just imagined to the *polis*

---

11. The adverb *exaiphnes* usually signals the inexplicable, traumatic turns in Platonic discourse. Paradigmatic passages in this sense are *Symposium* 210e and *Republic* 515c, 621b.

as he knows it, and from a healthy condition to a feverish one. He does it not to stir controversy, but because he needs to link the conversation to his own experience, and the city Socrates has so far delineated is unknown and unthinkable to him. He has never seen anything of the kind.

This is why Glaucon asks to see a "city of pigs"[12]—that is, a city nourished by much richer cuisine in addition to bread and wine. It is interesting (and symptomatic) that scholars and translators should concur in considering the reference to pigs as regarding the first city, the peaceful and amicable one, which would have to be deemed crudely primitive. But both the syntax and the general sense dictate that the pigs are rather the inhabitants of the second *polis*—the one Glaucon wants to see considered—because of the instinctiveness and intemperance with which they pursue their appetites. Not recognizing the subtlety and sagacity intrinsic to the first city, and thereby bringing it back to the image of a pig farm, reveals a most eloquent prejudice: that peace is, at bottom, boring, uninteresting; that friendly harmony is a form of monotony, when not of coarse simplicity; that nothing happens in this community that eschews excesses and articulates even transcendence, even the contact with nature and the divine, through a careful valuation of balance. It is as though, according to this prejudice, binging and debauchery would demonstrate cultural refinement, as though rough voracity and lack of proportion were felicitously dynamizing elements.

Be that as it may, with his intervention Glaucon introduces into the examination of the *polis* the bare and raw fact of a desire that devours, inside and out. He thereby imposes the confrontation with rampant needs. War makes its entrance at this point: in the city that now burns with fever, the inhabitants will desire more and more acquisitions, until the resources of the community and territory will no longer suffice and, in an uncontainable surge of avid anxieties, we will have to go and get those of our neighbors. And they, in turn, will do the same with us. Such is the origin of war, Socrates observes, and Glaucon has nothing to object: if that's the way it is, so be it.[13] Henceforth, solidarity will not be extended to human beings as such, the inhabitants of this or that *polis*, but only to fellow citizens with whom the longings for conquest are shared, to the detriment of foreign enemies. Friendship within, war without.

War thus becomes inevitable if the city must obtain energy and resources perceived to be insufficient. Not that they *necessarily* are

---

12. Plato, *Republic* 372d.
13. Plato, *Republic* 372a–373e.

insufficient—but perception of their scarcity is produced in the altered perception of needs (the superfluous becomes necessary), and hence in the transformation of consumption habits. It is notable that war is not essentially traced back to questions of identity and difference, which will appear on this scene only later. Here the problem is posed in terms of a limitless acquisitive impulse. (I recall, in my first winter in New York, a stroll up to Times Square. A slogan stood out, scrolling and flashing, that repeated, "Too much is never enough.") Thus emerges the problem of measure, now as well as then: the difficulty of admitting it, of measuring oneself against it, against the fact of finitude and, ultimately, of mortality and death.

But how, concretely, is one to distinguish excess, measurelessness, superfluity, luxury, and lust from measure and from necessity? Where is one to draw the limit, to acknowledge the point, the moment at which one should stop, once desire has been triggered and so, too, the mechanism of production? For, of course, it is not a matter of limiting oneself to necessity understood as a support of bare survival: being a human being has always already meant opening oneself up and unfolding beyond merely biological maintenance and species preservation. Then, if this is the case, how should we comprehend creativity, the need for novelty, the impulse ever to go further, while trying to outline the critique of a lifestyle that can only be upheld through aggression and destructiveness projected outside?

And furthermore, why does that which we recognize as necessary tend, by definition, to seem insufficient to us? Could it not, perhaps, appear *more than sufficient,* even *abundant* (as when what is given to us is enough, gives us joy, and we feel profound gratitude for it)? And why, on the contrary, does excess seem necessary, indeed both necessary and impossible ("Too much is never enough")? In the platonic pages we are reading, investigating human nature entails examining the enigma of human measure.

Let us also add, albeit briefly, reading Plato as we are trying to do here—emphasizing the psycho-political, and thus ethical, motives—involves a disempowerment (if not an eclipse) of more formalistic, epistemological, or "metaphysical" interpretations. The Platonic invitation to a certain detachment from materiality (from the urge to possess it, from identification with it, from obsessive involvement in acquisitive dynamics), presents a political relevance, well before and beyond announcing the separateness of earthly life from the hyperuranium. Prior to concerning a hypothetical domain of immobile and eternal ideas beyond the sky, with no link to the world of becoming, the philosophical path (the search for the good, toward the good) pursues peace and protects its possibility. That is to say, if peace is really what we want, inside and outside, it is necessary to heal, to set in order our relation to matter—it is necessary *to fast*.[14] The alternative to this is presented in the exemplary figure of the tyrant (examined, in particular, in Book IX), the extreme case of avidity, at once psychologically dismembered and fomenter of wars, which are the essential tool for the maintenance of one's own way of life, regardless of other(s).

Receptivity

Socrates recognizes Glaucon's intervention, his request for a discussion more adherent to their familiar circumstances, and grants the development that leads from the first, peaceful *polis* to the sick one. It will no longer be possible to retrace their steps, after such a decision, and the first city will no longer be remembered explicitly, even if it will remain an indelible reference for every aspiration to balance and health. The dialogue will now concern itself with the decadent city, which in everything resembles Athens. But it will also try to contain its excesses, to reorder it. The dialogue thus becomes an analysis and a therapy of contemporaneity.

Socrates proves to be capable of listening, although this will carry him far from his first evocations, forcing him to contradict positions he previously held—in particular, the affirmation that it is *never* just to harm anyone, be they friend or foe (*Republic* I).[15] The city that lives in peace, just like the world it anticipates, must be deserted. But what else could Socrates do? Continue with a monologue, having lost the engaged attention of the young interlocutors who are incapable of relating to his visions? Continue in what would then become a self-referential fantasy? For the love of dialogue, Socrates permits the interruption on Glaucon's part and absorbs the impact. He understands that Glaucon's objection stems from attention and interest in the subject, and not from sterile

---

14. I borrow this expression from Umberto Curi, *Terrorismo e guerra infinita* (Troina, Italy: Città Aperta Edizioni, 2007).
15. There is possibly reason to attribute particular importance to Book I of the *Republic*, if indeed its late drafting is assumed. See Erwin Rohde, *Psyche. Seelencult und Unsterblichkeitsglaube der Griechen* (1890–1894), *Psyche: The Cult of Souls and Belief in Immortality among the Greeks*, trans. W. B. Hillis (London: Kegan Paul, 1925), 477–479.

penchant for strife. He intuits the attentive enthusiasm, the *eros* that animates the young aristocrat, and glimpses its great formative potential.

After all, Socrates himself knows philosophy as folly and enamored rapture, as an effort sustained by the energy of desire (*Phaedrus*). While Cephalus ("the authority," "the head"), Polemarchus's father and owner of the house, had boasted about his "freedom" from desires in virtue of advanced age (*Republic* I), Socrates is a figure of desiring; his freedom does not entail the dimming of desire. While for Cephalus peace is reached in old age, in the weakening of vigor, Socrates will show how philosophical exercise and the peace (the healing) to which it aspires are a matter of passion, *pathos*.

For now, however, the consequences of the heed paid to Glaucon are clear: the *polis*, in its structure, comes to include the inevitability of war. Now, besides those who produce and possess material wealth, the city will need a class of guardian-warriors, and finally a class of more authoritative men and women providing laws and overseeing education. The Socratic proposal of an origin untouched by conflict and its causes seems to be reduced to almost nothing. It soon had to give way to the peremptoriness of things as they are.

And yet this "almost nothing" is not exactly nothing. And this "not nothing" proves to be notable for its influence and persistence. In virtue of this, the inevitability of the decadent and bellicose *polis* is not so obvious: the trace of an other community, at once evanescent and indelible, continues to disturb the presumed unavoidability of conflict. In and of itself, the passage from the first to the second *polis* seems indeed to be due more to dialogical exigencies (trying not to lose the attention of the young interlocutors) than to a metaphysically understood necessity. And this always characterizes discourse in dialogical form, which is never an abstract treatment of themes, but reflects the concrete circumstances of conversation; and which, above all, does not resort to external, allegedly objective reasons, verifications, and evaluations, but unfolds only thanks to the participants' convergence, requires only their accord to proceed.[16]

From the end of Book II to Book V, it will therefore be a matter of a tripartite *polis*: a war machine. The description of the intermediate class, that of the warriors guarding the city and fighting for it, moreover, brings about a curious ambiguity in the definition of philosophy. It is said that the guardians must be, like dogs, capable of aggression toward

---

16. Plato, *Republic* 348a–b.

the foreigner and of mildness toward their own fellow citizens. In this sense, their nature is said to be philosophical: they discern the known from the unknown, and love and regard as a friend (one of us, "at home with us") whomever is known, while they hate and regard as an enemy whomever is unknown.[17] This argument sheds light on the important nexus between aversion and ignorance, but, at the same time, plays on the strange confusion between the love of the known and the love of knowing. The latter, love of knowledge, never ends in static fixation on what is known: as a transformative endeavor, in an ongoing fashion it turns the unknown into the known, brings the previously foreign into the sphere of my acquaintance. The love of knowledge is altogether removed from the posture entailing love of the known and hostility to the unknown. In fact, it is so far from such a posture that the awareness of the unknown nourishes it, rather than constituting a threat for it. The love of knowing belongs to what still abides unknown and reaches out to it. Only in this latter sense does it seem possible to speak of philosophy: an exploration that tends to amplify itself, dynamizing the categories of the known and the unknown, thereby eroding and destabilizing the bases of enmity and hate. The unknown is loved for love of knowing.

EXERCISE OF PHILOSOPHY

Precisely such an amplifying operation is what we see enacted in Book V. After having developed, in detail, a *polis* whose *raison d'être* is the aggression of the surrounding communities, or at least the readiness to fight, Socrates imperceptibly effects a slippage in the interpretation of the figures of friend and enemy, own and other, proper and improper. As though following a trajectory that leads back to the positions left behind with the first city, he expands the sense of friendship while narrowing that of enmity. Increasingly more types of conflicts, even those between different cities, are condemned by him as factious (as civil wars, against "one's own"). War in the strict sense (against the alien), which initially pitted the city against anyone and anything outside its bounds, now designates belligerence between the Greek world as a whole and barbarians. Within the Greek world, everyone is alike, and it thus seems aberrant to consider one another enemies: in this way, the sense of cohesion and friendship is extended from the individual city to an entire constellation of culturally similar political bodies. If the logic of such a progression

---

17. Plato, *Republic* 376a–c.

were to be brought to its furthest consequences, one would eventually reach an understanding of humanity as such as "our own"; in that sense, every war would be a civil war. Socrates says, "And as Greeks, they won't ravage Greece or burn houses, nor will they agree that in a given city all are their enemies—men, women, and children—but rather that the enemies responsible for discord are always a few. And because of this, since the majority are friendly, they won't ravage the land or destroy houses; and they'll keep quarrelling only until those who are responsible for it will be forced to pay the penalty by those who are not responsible and suffer from it."[18]

Socrates's peculiar language is worth noting: considering a *polis* against which one could be at war, he does not refer to the inhabitants generically, as citizens or population. He speaks instead (and this is very unusual) of men, women, and children, and recognizes their friendship. The gaze becomes more comprehensive and detailed, consciousness succeeds in including and integrating ever more distant phenomena, precisely thanks to this drawing closer, to this looking ever more closely, putting minute phenomena into focus. This broadening that is also a drawing together allows us to recognize the neighborhood of those who live elsewhere, the communion and proximity of those who are apparently foreign. It makes possible a more intimate knowledge even of those whom we will never know: because we know their sorrow, we feel it in the fiber of our embodiment, in the most hidden receptacles of our being, if we stop to consider their situation. We feel that the feeling is shared, shared is the condition of precariousness.

It is this awareness that inhibits us in our military operations, Socrates says, so much so that we will establish laws to prohibit destructions, so that the many will not have to suffer the consequences of the acts of a few among them.[19] It is also interesting to note that, with implacable coherence, Socrates is here still responding to the opinions initially reported by Glaucon, according to which it would be best, if at all possible, to perpetrate injustice without having to pay the consequences. The man who is "truly a man" would choose to do this. What Socrates wishes for,

---

18. Plato, *Republic* 471a–b.
19. On the relation between intimacy with the other and conflict resolutions, I limit myself to mentioning Judith Butler, *Precarious Life: The Powers of Mourning and Violence* (New York: Verso, 2006); Julia Kristeva, *Strangers to Ourselves*, trans. Leon S. Roudiez (New York: Columbia University Press, 1991).

instead, is an awareness belonging to the many, such that those who are responsible for war and its destructions must necessarily make amends. Here as elsewhere Socrates demonstrates an extremely subtle transgressive potential, directed not at negating but at reconfiguring the values of masculinity and courage.

Those who drag an entire community into war for their own interests are a few. They are able to capitalize on common weaknesses and enchant, deceive, with no scruples manipulate the most obvious vulnerabilities. Profiting on the lack of emotional training and education of desire—in fact, favoring the scarcity of such a cultivation—the few instrumentalize the passions of the many. These are the enemies who undermine every community from within. They are enemies of humanity itself, its greatest denigrators, and not only enemies of a political organism, be it a *polis* or nation-state. This is why it should not be by external interferences that they should be brought to pay for what they have caused, but rather by their own fellow citizens.

It is already clear, then, that war classically understood (that is, war according to Hobbes, but also according to Books II–IV of the *Republic*—where, in a strict sense, war designates hostility between different states or *poleis*) is no longer possible. If the enemy does not coincide with a readily identifiable political body, one can no longer speak of war—or, at the very least, war must be radically rethought. To provide an example close to us: it has been observed many times that one of the first wars of the early 2000s, "the war on terror," was not based on a symmetrical confrontation between political bodies, but rather was declared against an enemy that was nebulous by definition, and became itself indistinct—to the point of losing the precision of contours and turning into an indefinite hostility, dangerously devoid of spatial and temporal limits. Yet one cannot fail to remember the discomfort of the US administration, consistently anxious to bring the situation back to familiar military schemas and national paradigms—for example through the identification of the enemy with "rogue states" converging into an "axis of evil." Indeed, it becomes improbable to wage a war against an enemy who subtracts itself and hides, and who cannot even be thought of simply as external to state borders: an internal enemy, between us and among us. Many events in our own times make all of this dramatically clear.

With the unhinging of the categories of friendship and enmity, then, Socrates seems to be searching for a way back, a reconnection with the positions left behind at the beginning of the dialogue. But Glaucon interrupts him anew. "Let us concede this and what was said before," he says, "but I think, Socrates, that if we were to let you go on speaking about such matters, you would never remember what you set aside earlier in order to say all this. That is to say: is it possible for a constitution" such as the one we have been discussing "to come into being, and in what way would it be possible?"[20] Glaucon thus calls Socrates back to the task they took up, thereby inhibiting his unanticipated and unplanned diversion. Is this *polis* possible—this *polis* first admitted in its feverish immeasurability and then cultivated and subjected to measurement? This is what Glaucon wants to know.

In Book V, therefore, the expansion of friendship beyond the borders of the single *polis* is limited to the confines of the Greek world. On the one hand, as has already been said, this expansion of the visual field calls the category of enmity itself into discussion. On the other hand, however, this operation tends to substitute the cohesion of the *polis* as a functional unity with a bond based on the recognition of common cultural traits, along the lines of the Amphictyonic league and such experiences of political and strategic alliance. This alters the perception of the causes of conflict: the war that still remains, that still bears the name of war (that between Greeks and barbarians), would now seem to be sparked not so much by a collective project of conquest and material acquisition, as previously highlighted, but by issues of belonging, identity, and linguistic and spiritual communion.[21] Although belated and derivative, this motive tends to establish itself in its conspicuity and to eclipse the first, favoring the more fortunate cliché according to which difference, and not the tyrannical *imperium* of unbridled desires, would be the basic motive of hostility.

One more word on the "barbarians." They are those with whom one communicates only with the greatest effort, if at all, and who remain distant, incomprehensible in their customs: as though the linguistic barrier obstructed as well the capacity to interact on other levels, semiotically and symbolically, recognizing one another in the same *pathos*. And yet, Socrates had gone down to the port—a place of exchange, ferment, and innovation—because he was curious to "see" the festivities held for the first time in honor of the foreign goddess. He had gone in order to *see up close*, and it seemed to him that the rituals organized by his fellow citizens and by the Thracian guests (at the limits of the "Greek world" and its language) were equally worthy. Although broken, the trajectory that extends the meaning of friendship beyond a single Greek city hints at an unstoppable movement beyond Greece itself and the Greeks. The

---

20. Plato, *Republic* 471c.
21. Plato, *Republic* 470e.

philosophical movement testifies to this. It challenges unrelentingly the contours of the known by opening up to the unknown, and, indeed, defends the possibility of what is not or is not yet, even though this possibility could bear fruit elsewhere in space and time. It is precisely in responding to Glaucon's pressure regarding the feasibility of the constitutional arrangement described in the dialogue that Socrates introduces again the question of the alien, denying that the philosophical Muse is a Greek prerogative. We are in Book VI:

> Then, if in the infinite past that went by, those who were prominent in philosophy necessarily had to take care of the city; or if even now there may be such a necessity in some place, among barbarians, well beyond our gaze; or if such a necessity will manifest itself later on, at any rate we are ready to defend our thesis, that the constitution we discussed here was, is, and will come to be when this Muse will be authoritative in a city. For it is not impossible that this should happen, we are not speaking of impossibilities. That this is difficult, we too agree.[22]

The wide-open view of the human being and of their potentiality (*dynamis*), of what they can do, be, and become, makes it possible not only to glimpse a hitherto unimaginable community, but also to consider it as such not impossible. The exploration of the possible transgresses and overturns the borders of the known.

REASON AND SENSIBILITY

The Books that follow (VI–IX) expose a formidable critique of reason in its presumed autonomy and indifference with respect to the world. In particular in Books VI and VII, we witness a threefold problematization of the possibility of science (of purely rational knowing). We will not be able to follow, here, its developments—particularly noteworthy for their recourse to an ever more evocative and figurative language that illuminates the physicality, the sensible relief of *logos*. Let us recall only its crucial moments: (1) the good, excessive with respect to the intelligible, is revealed through the analogy with the sun; (2) the discourse on the sensible and the intelligible (the divided line) emphasizes their continuity and interpenetration;[23] (3) the image of the cave, in the end, articulates the

---

22. Plato, *Republic* 499c–d; *Symposium* 209d–e.
23. This is the reading supported by Hermann L. Sinaiko, *Love, Knowledge, and Discourse in Plato* (Chicago: University of Chicago Press, 1965). See, too, John Sallis, *Being and Logos* (Bloomington: Indiana University Press, 1996).

ascent from the sensible to the intelligible, but anchoring it completely in the sensible order, and therefore drawing a circle (ascending motion, always already bound to a return) more than a simple rectilinear vector.

Within the glow of reason is an ineliminable moment of darkness; or, better, the very sense of reason as light is sustained by the light of phenomena. A purely rational approach, deprived of the contribution of sensibility, then, proves to be inaccessible. This is precisely why, in Book VIII, the decadence of the *polis* constructed during the dialogue is announced: as all things come to be and perish, so too will this *polis*, and similarly every construction that aspires to an immutable ideality.

Avidity, the anxious hunger for possession and accumulation, are that which first provides the impulse for the *polis*'s corruption, and then precipitate the situation into an unmanageable process of deterioration. As we noted before, they are the driving engine of war, disorder inside and out. In the figure of the tyrant we encounter the utmost expression of inner discord that, invested with worldly power, projects itself into external devastation.

If the difference between those who love knowledge (the philosophers) and those who possess it (the philosopher-kings) was announced already in Book V, following the examination of reason in Books VI–VII—and, in particular, after the drama of the cave—it emerges with increasing clarity that the philosopher (as is clear in the figure of Socrates) is not so much one who knows, but one who, driven by desire, pursues knowledge. Therefore, the therapy for the extreme human and political malady—tyranny—cannot entail the repressive contrast between reason and irrationality: the philosopher him- or herself is erotically motivated, and certainly no less implicated than others in the dynamics of appetites and impulses. Here, two big themes are delineated: in the first place, the tension between different modalities of desire; and then, the matter of ineludible desire, of the ineludible (as well as disturbing) instinctive contents, of which dreams are the evidence.[24] But the discernment of various types of desire, just like the cure for imbalances and discords in desiring, happen through a process that is itself essentially desiderative and implicated in corporeity. Of this process, the tyrant is the deviation and the shadow.

The greatness of Book IX—the book of the analysis of desires—consists precisely in this. We have no way of following its utterly

---

24. Plato, *Republic* 572b.

noteworthy *incipit*, here, but let us recall at least that it shows how philosophical research is itself situated in the context of care for the body and for the passions, and necessarily presupposes this care. If recognized, understood, and rightly nourished, desiring allows "the best part" to remain "pure and alone by itself, to go on investigating and yearning for the sensible perception of something it does not know, something that was, or is, or will be."[25] The lucid conjunction of sensibility and knowing is thus elaborated further. Ready to lay down to sleep, those who have cared for themselves in this way can "set in motion" what is "better," and rest: "You know," concludes Socrates, "that in such a state he more than ever grasps the truth, and in this moment the lawless visions appear in his dreams less."[26] It is, therefore, in sleeping and dreaming, when the body is finally at rest, that we can be otherwise awake and active, and what is true can present itself to us.

Dreams

Socrates therefore knows how to heed desires: but out of love for what can arise and come about whenever they have been understood. That is to say, he understands desires as essential elements in an ampler context that embraces them. In precisely the same way, Socrates knows how to listen to the companions who held him back at the port, in the nocturnal dialogue: out of love for what can take place whenever they may have been attentively followed. Despite appearances, Socrates never abandoned the vision of a just community, of a just way of living. He continued to feed it in silence, even while it seemed that his concessions to his interlocutors had completely distanced him from it. Instead, it is he who distances the young friends from the cultural desert in which they languish, so as to awaken their attention and imaginative impulse. At the end of Book IX it becomes evident that, through the long conversation, nothing has been obtained but the capacity to look up and see the sky, which was not possible at the beginning of the dialogue, and still not possible for the prisoners at the bottom of the cave. This possibility alone was worth the long exercise, for "in the sky, perhaps, there a paradigm is laid out for those who want to see and, seeing, dwell in themselves."[27]

Founding in oneself the city dictated in the sky—that is, living a life that has its roots in the sky—this is the possibility that philosophical

---

25. Plato, *Republic* 571e–572a.
26. Plato, *Republic* 572a–572b.
27. Plato, *Republic* 502b.

exercise finally allows one to glimpse. And it is with an evocation of the sky, of its resounding and dazzling composition, that Book X (and therefore the *Republic*) closes: looking at and listening to the sky, its splendor and music, for there is no beyond, no place beyond the place embraced by the sky, in which ideas could rest forever. There is only the sky, above and around us all: one, even if never the same. There is the earth. And there is what circulates between the one and the other.

Socrates thus tells of Er, who died in war and traveled in the company of "many others," all of them caught within the exchanges between life and death: Er, a human being so unique as to be "of all people" or "of all tribes" (*pamphylos*)—that is, such as to be a human being above all else, utterly singular, individuated in the sense of enacted as an individual, exceeding with respect to any category and belonging. His crossing of the sky is not resolved into a transcendent contemplation. Er returns from this vision and narrates it to the living: he reports what he has heard and seen in following those who come from life and those who prepare to return to life—in following the vast movements between death and life, the invisible transitions and the mechanisms that sustain reembodiment. He thus turns to life—this life—showing how it is inscribed within laws vaster than human decrees and how, in its unfolding from moment to moment, from one choice to the next, it could contribute to the life of the whole.[28] His is a story about how it is perhaps possible to choose, and therefore live, well. For it is choice that ongoingly shapes life in its permanent transiting and in its demeanor; it is choice (the passage at once fragile and decisive that is fulfilled at every instant) that constitutes the fiber of life.

Between sky and earth, between life and death, Er warns of the task and danger of choice—and not only the choice between one life and another, the choice of the next life in which one will be incarnated, but also and above all the choice that, right here, opens up every moment to that which is to come.[29] Philosophy as dialogue color-shifts into a contemplation that lives and gives shape to life.

---

28. Plato, *Republic* 618b–619b.

29. I have encountered the myth at the end of the *Republic* a number of times, discussing at further length what is here exposed very concisely. To give but a couple of references: Claudia Baracchi, "Exile in the Flow of Time: On Memory and Immortality in Plato's *Republic*," *Research in Phenomenology* 47, no. 2 (2017): 204–219, and Claudia Baracchi, "Animals and Angels: The Myth of Life as a Whole in Plato's *Republic* X," in *Plato's Animals*, ed. Michael Naas and Jeremy Bell (Bloomington: Indiana University Press, 2015), 209–224.

7. FRIENDSHIP AND POLITICS

A Comprehensive Vision

Aristotle, too, associates friendship with justice. At first he does so in a purely evocative way, but the implications of his gesture are already discernible: friendship will be a constant point of reference in his attempt to think through the nature and deep root of human coexistence, the form of its errant, uneven development. We have already mentioned this passage: "In travels, too, one may observe how close and dear every human being is to another. And friendship seems to hold a *polis* together, too, and lawgivers seem to pay more attention to friendship than to justice; for concord seems to be rather like friendship, and they aim at this most of all, and try to expel factious discord, which is enmity; and when human beings are friends they have no need of justice, while when they are just they need friendship anyway, and what is most just is held to be enacted in a friendly manner."[1] Traveling is here a figure of the human condition: nomadic, migrant, restless. Not unlike those who go by sea, by desert, or by inhospitable lands, wandering and relentless, human beings cross life. They sense the dangers that are an integral part of their earthly transit and they share among themselves the same vulnerability with respect to the boundless and the nonhuman. That is why,

---

1. Aristotle, *Nicomachean Ethics* 1155a21–29.

encountering one another or traveling together, they feel a familiarity toward each other, and are dear to one another. They sense a common belonging. They regard one another, reciprocally, with understanding and sympathy. Precisely in confronting the unknown, insidious possibilities, and wandering across strange places, they feel, more than ever, their closeness and similarity with respect to those who cross paths with them or travel with them: my neighbor, my semblance. This closeness is therefore not mere spatial contiguity, nor is similarity mere mirroring. Friendship is, first and foremost, the name of an elementary feeling, of a solidarity that comforts, accords, connects in sensing and thinking. And a harmonized and concordant community becomes imaginable, even at an immense distance.

Thus, precisely while explicitly affirming that friendship surpasses justice to the point of rendering it obsolete, or even unnecessary (friends "have no need of justice"), Aristotle elaborates friendship in terms of political cohesion—that is, ultimately, of justice. On the one hand, friendship exceeds justice; on the other, justice is realized in friendship and finds its greatest fulfilment therein. This apparent ambiguity is due to the broad semantic range of the two terms, friendship and justice, in Aristotelian discourse. Friendship transcends justice and exposes it in its subsidiarity, if by justice we understand the system of laws, the juridical instrument, and the subsequent order. This is one of the interpretations that Aristotle gives of justice. But he also speaks of justice as the complete and perfected gathering of human excellences, enacted toward the other and therefore at work in collective dynamics. In this latter sense, we can better understand its overlap with friendship. And yet, friendship as tender intimacy between excellent individuals and friendship as genuinely political bond are not the same thing. And it must be difficult to think them together, if it is true that their interweaving, which indicates the difference but also the indivisibility of ethics and politics—that is, of private and public—has almost disappeared from the thought and sensibility nearer to "us moderns."

Beyond the Law

To the extent that it never coincides with the text of laws, but rather abides as an orienting principle toward which the human infinitely stretches out, justice goes on to blossom in friendship. Both indicate what favors the harmonious cohesion of the *polis* and therefore display the same range: "In each form of constitution friendship is involved to the extent that justice is."[2] On the other hand, and in a perfectly coherent way, friendship far exceeds justice understood in a narrower sense, as legality. The juridico-normative system guarantees stability and protects the *polis* from dissent and discord: in this sense, justice is necessary for the institution and the subsistence of the *polis*. But complete friendship—the one that does not pursue further ends, and desires and rejoices in the good of the other—surpasses such a logic of bare survival. It embellishes life, transforms living into living well. It is easy to see, in these friendly relations, how juridical measures and the whole legislative effort become somehow superfluous, or how their functions are radically altered.

If friendship in the complete sense were prevalent, the justice that human beings continue asymptotically to approximate would be realized along with it. With this, justice as a system of juridical institutions would be supplanted. This is the open horizon, the vision of an experience that has hitherto never taken place. And yet, through the texture of past and present, as though in transparency, Aristotle allows this possibility to be glimpsed, precisely in its fragile status of possibility, an exceedingly thin thread within the weaving of time. This, too, suggests that politics as constitution and juridical institution is not coeval with friendship, but precedes it. It is necessary precisely to the extent that the condition of friendship is not a given—that is, to the extent that the members of the community do not stay together thanks to a predominantly friendly bond, in the happiness of con-sent, sensing together and assenting to each other. Above we saw that friendship in its fulfillment and perfection is a "rare" phenomenon indeed. Nevertheless, its sporadic incidence can function as a reminder and even as a promise, even if fragmentary and difficult to decipher: a promise of justice that is not yet and that remains to come, of a justice toward which human beings continue to tend, beyond legal codification.

In a certain sense, then, politics is a condition of friendship: it provides the setting, the context, in which friendship becomes possible. In its turn, friendship indicates the end or destination of politics, and thus its possible transcendence. In this way, too, their interdependence is manifested.

Friendship would therefore indicate the politics to come, no longer or not only based on the institution and implementation of rules. This is

---

2. Aristotle, *Nicomachean Ethics* 1161a10–11.

its visionary dimension. It allows for the imagination that a plurality of individuals may subsist and harmonize beyond legal prescriptions: no longer, not only, a community collectively and individually dominated by fear of the other and of violence at the hands of the other, and thus by the urgency of defending "one's own" (one's own possessions, one's own relatives, one's own environment), but instead a convening of individuals who choose each other and recognize each other, desiring their reciprocal good, in a broad perspective of further development. In the politics in the process of perfecting itself, precisely this evolution of motivation would be at stake: from self-defense, from preventative protection, to a unitive openness—free, desirous, loving.

Such a completion could be announced (we cannot here speak of realizing it) when being together, initially perceived in its unarticulated factuality (the fact of "traveling in the company of many"),[3] were to begin to fuel awareness of a more profound and significant sharing. It would come to be announced if the bare necessity of being-together were to become more spacious, allowing one to intuit that the other, the others, all of them just like us undergo the same conditions; if, that is, necessity were to provide a view such as to promote compassion, the acknowledgment of a shared suffering, of a common *pathos*. It would be a matter of consciously taking note of what always already is the case, awakening to the originary condition of being in the company of others, letting such a condition become (perhaps suddenly) noteworthy, significant, although at first it may have remained, all in all, insignificant, or rather inconspicuous. The seed of the transfiguration of politics into friendship would be found in this mindful waking up to interdependence.

It must be said, at least in the margins, that perhaps nothing could prevent such a transfiguration from being destabilizing, even potentially destructive, since friendship in its "perfect" sense seems to imply the obsolescence of political structures as we know them, and so of the stability these guarantee. In this sense, love or friendship could even constitute a threat to civil coexistence as it has been historically handed down. These are scarcely defined scenarios to our inquiring gaze—above all to the gaze of political thought—and yet robustly rooted in our experience. As we have seen, Aristotle often employs the language of *philia* and that of *eros* interchangeably and, interrupting his elaboration of the themes of measurement, balance, and the mean (*mesotes*), characterizes

---

3. Plato, *Republic* 614c.

the amicable-amorous relation in extreme, hyperbolic terms: friendship or love exceeds and thus precedes the law. It is a principle on the hither side of the law and beyond it, literally out-law, uncontainable.

We should underscore again that the friendship in play in these brief digressions is friendship in its primary and complete sense, and not the one that Aristotle calls friendship "in virtue of an attribute"—that is, friendship by chance, by accident: the decisively less demanding relationship that brings together for the sake of pursuing concrete and definite ends. This latter includes relations motivated by various appetites, in search of pleasure, advantage, or material benefits. Even friendship "by accident" fosters political cohesion, but in an instrumental and thus ancillary way: it includes relationships that are highly conventional, ritualized, aimed at limited "goods" and interests, and does not contemplate the deep motivations for living together. The point is not that material or finite goods are not essential. Indeed, they are. The difference between friendship in its completeness and friendship in a derivative sense lies in the ability (or lack thereof) to grasp the broader reasons in the finite, and thus to place the contingent in an otherwise articulated context.

Similarly to Plato, Aristotle considers instrumental friendship to be truncated and impoverished.[4] On the contrary, as we shall see, he recognizes in complete friendship an excess certainly intractable (for it does not lend itself to control, be it conceptual, political, or normative), but also generative, rich in implications of extraordinarily vast consequence.

Benevolence

We saw above that benevolence is not friendship realized in its singularity. But it is its beginning, its *arche*. It could be said that benevolence is "potentially perfect" friendship, were this not a paradox, since the perfecting would consist precisely in the overcoming of potentiality through actualization, exercise, cultivation. And yet Aristotle says this: benevolence is perfect friendship, but without time and shared experience. It is "perfect" friendship but *arge*, not operative (not in *ergon*), and therefore

---

4. Suffice it to recall, here, Plato's treatment of *eros* in the first stages of the *Symposium* (178a–185c). If, on the one hand, paradigmatically in the figures of Phaedrus and Pausanias, *eros* is presented in the service of political functions, as a factor that in some ways promotes and favors optimal political dynamics, on the other hand the comprehensive structure of the Platonic dialogue clearly exposes the partiality and incompleteness of this view of love. Also, crucially: *Phaedrus* 256e–257a.

deprived of its energy: friendship that does not take place, friendship in principle, perhaps. In the other, I sense a possibility, a possible openness, the development of a possible interaction, even if I cannot (or do not want to, am not in the condition to) act on this possibility.

In the *Nicomachean Ethics*,[5] as in the *Eudemian Ethics*,[6] the phenomena of benevolence (*eunoia*) and concord (or communion in thinking, *homonoia*) are treated together and never neatly separated. We encountered, not long ago, a reference to concord in the initial passage of the discussion of friendship,[7] where Aristotle employs the term to describe the accord among travelers. We noticed, in that context, that concord, even before designating the unity and coherence of a political body (and, in this sense, exhibiting the same function as justice), indicates the primordial feeling of bonding and recognition, a feeling that characterizes not so much political aggregation in contrast to other *poleis*, but rather the human community as a whole and as such.

In the elaborations following the opening statement, concord comes to designate communion and commonality of intent, a shared point of view with regard to practical and political matters. This is what Aristotle calls "political friendship," *politike philia*.[8] Although benevolence and concord are not identical, they similarly refer to a bond that can in potency be in(de)finitely extended, all the way to faraway and unknown people. Even though partial, their overlap is an important fact: it suggests that benevolence (friendship "in principle"—that is, the origin and condition of perfect friendship) confers its character even on political friendship.

Benevolence is an elementary awareness that there are others, a togetherness of which I am a part, and, consequently, that there is a common good that concerns me, a common good inseparable from my good, in which my good is set. This awareness is a principle of friendship as a singular and always unique bond, but also of friendship as a political bond. In fact, therefore, benevolence shows that the experience of friendship, which in and of itself cannot be lived an infinite number of times, can nevertheless be universalized, transposed into the experience of a shared end and a collective, hence political, accord. It can be universalized without being thereby transformed into mere abstraction, because

---

5. Aristotle, *Nicomachean Ethics* 1166b30–1167b16.
6. Aristotle, *Nicomachean Ethics* 1241a1–34.
7. Aristotle, *Nicomachean Ethics* 1155a21ff.
8. Aristotle, *Nicomachean Ethics* 1167b2, 1241a33.

it is based on a primordial *pathos* that entails recognition, commonality, affection. In this sense, the phenomenon of *homonoia*, of concordant thought exercised in political deliberation, remains significantly bound to the matrix (to the *arche*) of complete friendship, in its character each time unique, lived, and hyperbolic. The continuity (and not the fracture) of public and private, ethics and politics, is then underscored even in this way. What binds me to the friend and what binds me to the community and makes me participate in a common world, come from one and the same root, display the same nature. This also means that what guarantees political cohesion is not some derivative expedient, some pretended measure meant to contain primordial forces that would push in a completely different direction. On the contrary, political cohesion is no less primordial, is not secondary to the bonds between and among individuals. It emerges out of the same background of human sympathy that grounds every microcosm, each individual friendship.

This should not surprise us. Already at the opening of his reflection on ethics, Aristotle explicitly posits that individual good and that of the *polis* are the same, except that the good of the *polis* is, literally, greater, and therefore more worthy of honor and attention.[9] But saying that the good for me and the good for all are one, means thinking the individual, the "I," not opposed to the "we," but actually belonging to the "we" in the sense that in the "we" it finds the conditions most favorable for realizing and disclosing itself. Therefore, it is in the "we" that I become more fully myself and find my freedom. The "we" is not the limit to my good that I must unfortunately observe, in order to "show respect" for the sphere of others, but rather is the very terrain of my flourishing. We see clearly how the very modern value of "tolerance," which would want to mitigate each individual's egoistic drive so as to render coexistence possible, is called into question. Tolerance makes sense only if the human being is understood as the wolf of which Hobbes speaks, which, left to itself, would do nothing but unleash its ferocity on whoever might enter its territory. It is far from established that things are indeed this way, for the human being, and it is not altogether clear why this perspective should be so automatically and uncritically accepted. What is established, from an ethological point of view, is that even for wolves, surely, things are not this way. But, in this light, tolerance seems to be nothing other than a remedy for evils of our own doing and our own invention.

---

9. Aristotle, *Nicomachean Ethics* 1094b8–11.

Although aware of the irreducible difference between "perfect" and "political" friendship, Aristotle all the same rejects their simple disjunction.[10] Sensing the importance of thinking these phenomena conjointly, he explores the *continuum* of friendship and, through benevolence, brings back the political relation to the experience of friendship between excellent human beings (the infinite impulse through finite conditions). This experience remains, for Aristotle, the root and the "measure" of the manifold phenomenology of friendship. In order to corroborate this point further, we should underscore that the same concord, *homonoia*, is conceived in reference to excellence: "Such concord is found in good human beings; for they have the same thoughts in relation both to themselves and to one another, and thus rest, so to speak, on the same; for the things desired by such human beings are constant and do not ebb and flow like water in the strait of Euripus, and they also desire that things be just and favorable, and these are the things they aspire to in common. But bad human beings, on the other hand, cannot have the same thoughts except to a small extent, just as they cannot be friends."[11] In the *Eudemian Ethics*, Aristotle is even more determined to grasp the dependence of *homonoia* on excellence or goodness: concord, he affirms, "is to be found in the case of good individuals."[12] Moreover, given that "apparently concord, just like friendship, may not be said simply," it follows that "its primary and natural manifestation is good, and therefore it does not happen that bad human beings may agree with each other in that way."[13] Not only, then, does Aristotle not oppose "perfect" friendship (narrowly conceived as a private affair) to "political" friendship (as an alliance based on ideological identification and aimed at public prosperity). Aristotle conveys that political friendship should be clarified with reference to the phenomenon of individual friendship, to that relationship in the context of which individuals can become fully themselves and exercise, magnify, further cultivate excellence and goodness. Nothing less. Political aggregation is illuminated by this basic experience, even though, in its hyperbolic character, such an experience cannot really provide intelligible paradigms for the construction of programs and ideologies.

---

10. The possibility glimpsed here is regularly negated. For instance, among more recent works, Alexander Nehamas, *On Friendship* (New York: Basic Books, 2016).
11. Aristotle, *Nicomachean Ethics* 1167b5–11.
12. Aristotle, *Eudemian Ethics* 1241a22.
13. Aristotle, *Eudemian Ethics* 1241a23–26.

Despite Carl Schmitt

The view of political space as essentially linked to the elementary and amorous experience of friendship (even if in its minimalistic version, as beneficial solidarity) stands in stark contrast to the thesis of Carl Schmitt, according to which the political would find in radical enmity its own condition of possibility, as well as its originary motivation. From Schmitt's perspective, friendship would be an accessory element to political cohesion—accessorial and derivative with respect to the primordiality of conflict.[14] Here, however, it is not so much a matter of setting forth a theoretical opposition, but rather of rejecting the alleged Greek ancestry of Schmitt's thought, and recovering, especially in the letter of the ancient texts (Platonic as well as Aristotelian), radically diverging perspectives on the question of the origin of the political.

Schmitt's interpretation attributes a purely ancillary function to political friendship, included within the friend/enemy opposition and subordinated to the priority of enmity. Friendship so understood has nothing in common with the loving relation, and is reduced to a mere defensive exigence against an enemy, who is always a "public" enemy. But on the threshold of the founding discourse in Plato's *Republic*, as we saw, the *arche* of the *polis* is not the constitution of a common identity (of a common posture) against an external enemy. The political origin is not articulated in a constraint called friendship, which institutes affinity, stringently holds individuals together in a collectivity, and obliges them to reciprocal defense and the protection of their interests, of their goods. We have already underlined this: in the Platonic text, the bond of friendship aimed at self-defense and at acts against a common enemy comes into play only later: war is secondary to political founding—hence, neither originary nor essential. Constitutive of the political dimension is rather the fact that, as Plato has Socrates say, everyone has many needs and is not self-sufficient.[15] Human beings meet and join together out of necessity, lack, inadequacy, on the ground of an implicit recognition of the vulnerability of each, and in the awareness, no matter how hazy, that together they can grow, live better. One of the tasks faced in the conversation is indeed to bring the "community of pleasures and pains" more sharply to consciousness.[16]

---

14. Carl Schmitt, *The Concept of the Political*, trans. G. Schwab (Chicago: University of Chicago Press, 2007).
15. Plato, *Republic* 369b.
16. Plato, *Republic* 464a.

The results of the foregoing analysis must be summarized: not only, in the *Republic*, does the friend/enemy dichotomy appear relatively late with respect to the founding phase of the political, but also, as soon as it is admitted, it begins to be gradually loosened, until it comes to be transcended anew. Through the progression of the dialogue, we first see the archaic city, which lives peacefully, interacting in a peaceful way with other cities. Only at a later stage does the unrestrained and senseless growth of appetites within the community lead to the decline of the first form of coexistence. At the same time, this development necessitates the introduction of war, for ever more resources are required, and the city must appropriate neighboring lands in order to procure them.[17] In Books II–V, the city-soul is thus outlined in its tripartite structure, according to the logic of friendship within, war without. Along this whole trajectory, one should notice the devastating critique that Plato aims at the logic and privilege of the institution of the family. Such a critique tends to shift the question concerning belonging, identity, and their axiological structure from the level of tribal conventions to that of being: ontological considerations, the very distinction between being and appearing, far from abstractly formal, become urgent precisely as an analytical, critical, and emancipative instrument with respect to the force of customs, of current opinions, and of the unthought in them.[18] The attempt, central in the dialogue, at illuminating justice "in the psyche"—that is, the just life—should be read in this key, since the just are not necessarily those who have the appearance of being just and are publicly recognized and honored as such.

But constituting a political organism in which the correspondence between institutional and psychic structures is stable and transparent will turn out to be impossible. That is, the limits, the nonomnipotence of the sovereign, of the philosopher-king, will be exposed: it will never

---

17. Plato, *Republic* 373d–e.
18. In *The Politics of Friendship* (1994), trans. G. Collins (London: Verso, 1997), Jacques Derrida maintains the contrary—namely, that it is the logic of fraternity, of blood ties, and of the friend/enemy dichotomy that symbolically and conceptually underpins ancient discourse. It is not easy to explain such a resoundingly missed encounter with ancient thought, especially on the part of a philosopher who has taught so many to think alterity, to sharpen the ear, to practice listening, often fathoming unheard-of vitality in the philosophical repertoires approached—in the texts in whose company we think. But the democracy to come, if and when it will indeed come, will not come without a profound upheaval in the relation that the living entertain not only with the unborn but also with the dead.

be sufficiently emphasized that the psycho-political constitution in the *Republic* undergoes, over the course of the dialogue, its own deconstruction, announced at the outset of Book VIII. Justice has not yet been done to the philosophical scope of this movement, to the profound sense of the Platonic gesture that consciously inscribes mortality in its own *logos*.

Ultimately, the logic of the city of friends, formed and unified through the conflict against the other, is superseded: the citizens of the other *poleis* against which the city can be at war are not, for the most part, enemies—those "men, women, and children" are "friendly," only a few among them must be held responsible, and therefore the destruction caused by war must be avoided.[19] The community to which one belongs becomes ever more inclusive: it casts out ever fewer enemies, its projection of enmity outside itself fades. This progressive broadening of the political organism culminates in the "cosmopolitan dream" of the final myth: the figure of Er suggests a human being so unique, so singular, as to be *pamphylos*, "of all tribes," no longer ascribable to any political, tribal, or territorial identification whatsoever.[20] Thus analyzed in its entire trajectory, Plato's text authorizes neither the ideology according to which political space would originate in conflict, nor the identification of amity and enmity, respectively, with residing on the hither side and residing on the other side of the border drawn—that is, with interiority and exteriority, sameness and alterity.

Nor, in the Aristotelian reflection considered above, did we find support for the thesis asserting political and individual bonds as clearly (that is, qualitatively) separated. In Aristotle we gathered cues for thinking about community, political togetherness, on the basis of the radically singular experience of friendship. The corporeal uniqueness of each friendship cannot provide a model reproducible on the level of political interactions; and yet, politics seems to be based on the universality of such a seemingly nonreplicable occurrence. It seems to presuppose that the experience of friendship, although different in each case, is precisely as such common—and available to human beings as such. It further presupposes that the feelings of sympathy and affection, which the individual cannot enact *ad infinitum*, are in principle infinitely extendable. Again, the universality of the unrepeatable.

Ancient thought does not understand political friendship only in terms of calculation and strategic alignment. Before all else, in political

---

19. Plato, *Republic* 471a–b.
20. Plato, *Republic* 614b.

friendship is revealed the possibility, in principle, of being together, of holding in common, sharing favors and projects. And, as concord, political friendship harbors in itself traces of perfect and singular friendship—that is, of the orientation to the good. Like justice itself, such friendship infinitely exceeds administrative or procedural concerns. And, after all, excess marks not only "perfect" friendship, but justice too. If justice unites thanks to the harmonization and the balance between giving and receiving,[21] it is nevertheless true that it does not limit itself to insisting on the restitution of what has been received. Aristotle says that human beings "situate the temple of the Graces in well visible places, so as to foster the return of what was given; for this is a sign of grace: we should return a service to the one who has shown grace, and then should take the initiative in showing it."[22] Beyond mere debt repayment, justice (and therefore the force and the constancy of a communitarian bond) indicates the willingness to give more, to give spontaneously, gracefully, without answering for a debt and without being forced to do so. Here we glimpse the free initiative of solidarity, the acknowledgment of a being together that far exceeds all computation. And solidarity confers a wholly other solidity on the *polis*, compared to the mere settling of accounts.

Thus, when Aristotle affirms that, if human beings were friends, justice (as a legal reference) would be superfluous, he imagines friendship as the end or destination of politics: as the highest political achievement. In this sense, friendship would mark the overcoming of politics as management program, as production of norms aimed at maintaining coexistence within tolerable parameters. It would mark the perfection of a politics to come, the harmonization of many, gathered electively, beyond duty. As if to say, politics is not "crowd management" but an evolutive possibility. The orientation to such perfecting would be announced precisely in friendship (in politics) as *homonoia*: nearness to others and awareness of a common belonging (as in the course of a journey), of shared circumstances, of mutual implication and interdependence.

In the folds of this vision of the possible, the end of politics is intuited as neither mere convenience nor the organization, ordering, and logistics of civil coexistence. Like friendship, politics, too, aims at happiness, living well, the flourishing of life in its manifold potential.

---

21. Aristotle, *Nicomachean Ethics* 1132b32–1133a3.
22. Aristotle, *Nicomachean Ethics* 1133a3–6.

Friendship and Cosmopolitanism

We have underscored many times the diverging paths of the ancients and the moderns. Particularly beginning with Kant, friendship and happiness slip to the margins of philosophical and political discourse, lose prestige in the public sphere, for in the meantime the separation between public and private has been consummated. Thus, friendship and happiness come to regard individual affairs—insular, heterogenous, essentially unrelated, politically irrelevant, when not perturbing. In the ancient Greek reflection things stand otherwise: especially in Aristotle we find, coherent and ubiquitous, the indication of a certain undecidability between public and private matters. The difference between these is never elaborated in terms of a split, opposition, or even relative autonomy. So, the pursuit of friendship and self-realization is certainly recognized in its always unique development, and yet this is never without political significance. Conversely, friendship, happiness, and living well, to be sure, are also understood in terms of political teleology, but this never means that individual becoming is or should be subjected to a homogenizing logic and resolved therein. Actually, in play here is a matter of great consequence: the whole (*holos*) is an open system, a welcoming (and not a fear) of differences, thanks to which it is enriched, discloses itself to the hitherto unseen, lives. In this light, politics is friendship with the unforeseeable.

It could be said that Aristotelian reflection provides resources for the systematic overcoming of the opposition between public and private, universality and singularity; that indeed, far from such a dichotomy, from the hierarchy it entails, and from its mere inversion, this reflection allows us to think universality *together* with singularity. It allows us to glimpse the universality of the singular: singularity—that is, the absolute irreducibility and irreplaceability—as what is shared, common, and, only in this sense, "universal." We could imagine, in sum, a commonality of radical uniqueness. Absolute singularity is not demoted to a declination of a universal paradigm, hence it does not fall into the universal-particular opposition; it lends itself neither to saying nor to thinking; it is not a "thing" that can be approached in the search for a definition ("what it is"); at most, it can be evoked through allusion, through imagination, poetically. And yet, what is elusive, what escapes reason and the question "what?," does not as a consequence amount to nothing. The vision of such a commonality may be a fertile contribution to the meditations on universalism and cosmopolitanism that have recently received renewed impetus (consider figures as diverse as Habermas, Derrida, Kristeva, Nancy—but also, first of all, Weil).

In the genealogy that goes from the Stoics to the Enlightenment and to Kant, cosmopolitanism has been thought on rationalistic grounds: it is as a rational subject that the human being can transcend material circumstances and recognize itself as a full-fledged citizen of the world, as a member of a community that has neither place nor territory. Of course, we should not oversimplify the many varied forms of rationalism. Of course, in Kant (unlike in the French Enlightenment tradition and in English empirical rationalism) reason articulates itself well beyond scientific discipline, to touch its own limits, and foretell its own overcoming: reason as a place of antinomies as well as rational subjectivity framed within freedom and the "kingdom of ends," mark the depth and complexity of this thought. Not to mention the *logos* of the Stoics, associated, as in Heraclitus, with the supreme god (Zeus) and his fire: "The all-pervading *logos*," says Cleanthes, "that mixes itself with the great star and the small ones."[23] Zeno of Citium refers to this mode of reason, at once cosmic and divine, in order to imagine a human community harmonized with the laws of nature.[24] Meanwhile Epictetus, in the all-pervasiveness of *logos*, will grasp the ground of a common sensing, of a sympathy among all forms of life—from vegetal life to the bodies of animals, to the celestial ones.[25] We can see clearly, here, that it is not a matter of forms of rationality that would be exhausted in calculation or in mathematical formalism.

But it is Aristotle who points to the possibility of a universal vision that does not rest on a rational foundation, however understood. The course of his thought mitigates the privilege of reason and allows us to think the global community of the human species without referring uniquely to rationality: to that rationality that makes us equal, and makes the community a multitude of equal unities, perfectly equivalent from a rational point of view. (After all, as the last century has shown, reason has not exactly evinced the authority and traction that every rationalistically inspired political theory wished to attribute to it.) Even before we share reason, we are brought together by vulnerability, exposure to the world and in the world, corporeal and sensible rootedness. Here, then,

---

23. Cleanthes of Assos, *Hymn to Zeus*, trans. E. H. Blakeney (New York: Macmillan, 1921), 12–13.
24. Diogenes Laertius, *Lives* VII.1.87–88.
25. Epictetus, *Discourses* (*Diatribai*) I.14.1–6.

is outlined an unheard-of universality: the universality of *pathos*. And here, too, is the possibility of understanding equality differently from equivalence: equality in the light of difference and incommensurability.

Especially in the light of the circumstances in which the new millennium opened, it seems imperative to learn to think human community in its entirety, without this entailing the elimination of differences, and without reducing the differences to identity-related and localistic velleities. The orientation of ancient thought that we have hitherto followed offers unexpected suggestions for conceiving of a human community neither according to the alleged neutrality of rationality, nor according to tribal and cultural identifications. It rather discloses the imagination of a community in which national and territorial belonging are recognized as crucial determinants of histories, lives, and individual identities, but without these determinations exhausting the infinitely variegated phenomenon of singularities: individuals becoming themselves, individuating themselves in their radically unrepeatable becoming. In other words, one can think of recognizing cultural and material bonds without transmuting them into forms of confinement and imprisonment—and, inversely, of conceiving freedom without transforming it into the predictability and in-difference of incorporeal rational subjects. One can begin to grasp the deterritorialization of the human, the deep truth of their nomadism, without falling back into strategies of abstraction and disembodiment, but rather perceiving acutely the suffering of their errancy.

One must insist on this: in this perspective, cosmopolitanism does not entail the exclusion of what is distinctive, what unutterably enfolds the unicity of each. And so, cosmopolitanism can be conceived in the light of corporeity and of the concomitant differences of sex, race, culture, religion, history, experience, social roles, and masks. It is not necessary to lose one's peculiarities, to abstract oneself, to be equivalent. The traits that individuate each of us can be exclusive without excluding. It would be a matter of refining the perception of difference, the experience of it: on the one hand, beyond the posture (or imposture) of individualism, provincialism, nationalism; and, on the other, beyond the universality that levels, annuls, and cancels out the discrepancies. One could thus, perhaps, heal these parodic deformations of the individual and the universal, and the wound of their dichotomy. One could, perhaps, begin to sense the community and not just think it—that is, to sense it even on the ground of affection, commotion, being moved together; to sense it not only on the basis of what we are, know, and possess, but of what we are not, do not know, do not possess.[26] Thereby announced would be a community, not only of identity, but also of that which, both inside and outside ourselves, remains strange and foreign to us—extraneous, estranged, disturbing, and perturbing—ultimately, *unheimlich*. Such would be (were it ever to be) the community of those who, as has been said, have nothing (almost nothing) in common—not in the sense that they share nothing, but in the sense that what they share (which is not nothing) is not their property, neither materially nor conceptually.

Were it ever to be, this would be the community of singularities who share, in each case, their singularity, even to the point of the unspeakable. Such a community would not imply a denial, a degradation, or a depreciation of reason, but rather the understanding that reason is not all-comprehending but, instead, itself comprehended; that reason is *never* given *as such*, but always filtered through life, with the inflections and deviations of the case; that reason is given through the life to which it necessarily belongs, through the space-time in which it is necessarily implicated. Consider the indefinite multiplicity of languages, reasons, paths, and routes that reason can, and in fact does, follow: not *logos*, but irreducibly *logoi*. Such would be the community of the infinite singularities that inflect common reason, that modulate reason, revealing its incompleteness (which then is a richness) and its essentially perspectival character.

---

26. Such would be the community of desire profiled in the Platonic *Symposium* (200e).

8. FRIENDSHIP AND NATURE

Asymmetry

As we have seen, equality and symmetry are not necessarily symptomatic of the perfection of friendship. Rapports driven only by dubious appetites or self-interest present the same symmetry characteristic of the most perfect friendship, the relatedness drawn to and by the good. The friends involved are in both cases equals, whether equally turned toward the good, or equally committed to less exalting endeavors. But Aristotle also includes under the heading of friendship relationships altogether other than symmetrical—relationships characteristically "uneven," connecting radically unequal beings. Such friendships are neither perfect nor imperfect, neither incomplete nor derivative. They just fall outside the paradigm (if it is one) of the friendship between or among equals considered so far.

Friendships involving inequality and asymmetry, and hence suspending or altering the requirements of reciprocation and mutual recognition, are far from relationships in a minor key, diminished, lacking, promoting banal advantages. Quite the contrary: they vividly illuminate the vertical energy of amity. They announce that friendship, varied and nuanced in its phenomenology, transcends the scenarios of "even" relations—relations between peers brought together by more or less felicitous inclinations, more or less fulfilled, attaining different approximations of perfection or failing altogether in that regard. Thus, after examining at length this mode of friendship, Aristotle turns to observe the various phenomena of "uneven" bonds that, as such, cross abyssal discontinuities and cast bridges between faraway shores. And here, in this other relating that binds dissimilar beings, turning them into friends, it becomes even more evident how friendship works at the articulation of the community of the world, weaving the bonds of solidarity in virtue of which the whole hangs together. If indeed it does.

Justice, too, is concerned with unequal relations—and not secondarily, but precisely in the perspective of an equalization through proportional and harmonious exchanges:

> In every community there seems to be something just, and friendship as well. At least human beings turn to their travel companions and fellow soldiers as friends, and they do the same also with those in any other community. Friendship extends as far as the community does, and likewise that which is just, too. And it was correctly said: the things of friends are in common; for friendship is in community. Brothers and comrades have everything in common, but others have only a few things in common, some more, some fewer things; for, even among friendships, some are more accomplished friendships, others less. And just things differ as well, for things that are just for parents toward their children and for brothers toward each other are not the same; nor are those among comrades the same as those among citizens, and similarly for other kinds of friendship. . . . What is just also increases by nature simultaneously with friendship, since they are in the same beings and extend in the same way.[1]

We note, here, the slippage from friendship based on similarity and equality to friendship between beings in various ways of unequal standing. The unequal is what friendship, as indeed justice, at once amalgamates and preserves as such. The second half of Book Theta is devoted to the analysis of friendship especially in terms of verticality, as a relation that holds together heterogenous beings, infinitely incongruent in their power, character, and qualities.

We will come to see this better: the elaboration of verticality will entail highlighting the relation between human beings (mortals) and gods (immortals) and, and the same time, the relation between human beings

---

1. Aristotle, *Nicomachean Ethics* 1159b27–1160a8.

and nature as such. At stake here, and especially set into relief, is the recognition of the political end (the end of the *polis* as well as of every community and commonality) beyond mere utility:

> Now all communities are like parts of the political community; for human beings travel together with a view to something advantageous and bring along something that contributes to life. The political community itself seems to have originated and still to subsist for the sake of advantage; for legislators, too, aim at this, and they say that what is usually advantageous is just. The other communities aim at some particular advantage, e.g. sailors undertake a voyage with a view to some profit or something like that, fellow-soldiers go to war with a view to plunder or victory or the taking of a city, and the same happens with the members of a tribe or a district.[2]

At first, Aristotle seems to interpret the end of politics in terms of expediency or common advantage. Nevertheless, he immediately adds that advantage (that which favors) should be conceived in its fuller meaning, as that which transcends partisan, ephemeral, and myopic concerns: "Some communities seem to be constituted for the sake of pleasure, as for instance religious guilds and clubs; for these come to be respectively for the sake of performing sacrifices and of companionship. All these seem, however, to be inscribed within the political community; for the end of the latter is not limited to present advantage but extends to life as a whole."[3] It is necessary to note the abundance of references through which the theme of political association is exposed. The prominence initially accorded to the useful is not altogether dropped, nor set aside. On the contrary, very significantly the language of the advantageous, the useful, the expedient, is preserved and exalted, displayed in its whole semantic spectrum, in an amplification that approaches a reconfiguration, or even a transfiguration. Extended to "life as a whole," capable of comprehending the human adventure in its long range, the perspective of advantage can no longer imply immediate gratification, nor the privilege of partial or unilateral undertakings. Advantage, instead, comes to embrace the highest end, in the most inclusive sense; and this is displayed precisely by associations that do not have "profit," "loot," or "victory" as their end, but rather the pleasure of staying together among fellows and

---

2. Aristotle, *Nicomachean Ethics* 1160a8–19.
3. Aristotle, *Nicomachean Ethics* 1160a19–23.

interweaving relationships with the dissimilar (for example, through the celebration of sacrifice). The trajectory of this discourse sheds light on political association as the network of relations in virtue of which life as a whole can be contemplated in its rhythm, articulation, and vastness.

This is reiterated even more incisively in the *Politics*, where Aristotle repeatedly affirms that political aggregation is ultimately oriented to living well and subsists for the sake of this;[4] whereas exchanges, the shared space, and defense against aggressions on the part of others, cannot of themselves explain the origin of the *polis*.[5] Of particular interest in the development of the passage here in question, however, is the powerful synthetic gesture through which Aristotle connects the issue of political end with themes concerning the divine and nature. The various associations that are parts of the comprehensive political association, Aristotle continues, "offer sacrifices and arrange gatherings for that purpose, assign honors to the gods and provide pleasant relaxations for their members. For the sacrifices and gatherings of the ancients, it seems, took place after the harvest, as a kind of first fruits, because in that season people had most leisure."[6]

The practice of sacrificing to the gods—that is, the bond between the human sphere and the divine one—is aligned with the bond between human beings and nature. Aristotle weaves together the rhythms of nature and those of humans: the cycles of the seasons, those bearing fruit and the barren ones, as well as the cycles of human labor and leisure. He presents nature as the theater of divine manifestation, as that which dictates the times of harvest, of gathering, of feasting, and of the ritual proper to humans. Here suggested is the convergence, if not simplistically the identity, of the relation with the natural and of the relation with the divine. The human is the place of this convergence, and from this convergence the human arises.

However, this gesture is not new to Aristotle. A passage in the *Protrepticus*, touching on the topic of contemplation, places the generation of the human in the merging (or even in the overlapping) of nature and the divine: "The human being is the most honorable of the animals in this world, so it is clear that the human was generated by nature and according to nature. What, then, is that for the sake of which nature and god have brought us into being? Asked what this end is, Pythagoras said

---

4. Aristotle, *Politics* 1280a32, 1280b34, 1281a2, 1281a3, 1328a37.
5. Aristotle, *Politics* 1280a32–39, 1280b30–35.
6. Aristotle, *Nicomachean Ethics* 1160a23–28.

'to contemplate the heavens'; and he used to say he was one who contemplates nature and because of this he had come into life."[7] The same hendiadyc formulation "nature and god" also appears in *De caelo*.[8] But let us observe more closely the interweaving of the bonds, not only horizontal, that involve the human animal "in this world."

Above and Below

In the context of these discourses we should recall, even only schematically, the Aristotelian hierarchy of relational forms and the corresponding forms of government.[9] First mentioned is the father-son relation, corresponding to the monarchical form of government; then, the husband-wife relation, corresponding to aristocracy; the relation between brothers, corresponding to timocracy; *demokratia* (which does not simply mean "democracy" in the modern sense of the term, but also "the power of the masses" in its degenerative aspects), which represents a debasement of the relation between brothers and so of timocracy;[10] oligarchy, which represents a corruption of the husband-wife relation and so of aristocracy; and, finally, the relation between master and slave, which corresponds to tyranny and represents a perversion of the father-son relation and of monarchy. We should notice the friction between the previous emphasis on the highest friendship that is realized between peers and the decisive downgrading, in this context, of peers' relation (the relation between two or more brothers). In fact, fraternity, the fraternal and horizontal relation between equals, be it in the "timocratic" or "democratic" version, does not enjoy any privilege here.

It seems important to underscore the significance of this transition. We can hypothesize that, with such a move, Aristotle is attempting to shed light on the limits of the fraternal relation as a paradigm of human community. This bond, based on the equal dignity, if not identity, of its members, is suggestive of a detachment with respect to alterity and the difficulties it poses. It is shielded from the heterogeneous. It can

---

7. Aristotle, *Protrepticus* fr. 11.
8. Aristotle, *Da caelo* 271a33. The human being at the confluence of natural and divine causes returns in the already quoted *Nicomachean Ethics* 1179b21–23. See also *Eudemian Ethics* 1216a11–16.
9. Aristotle, *Nicomachean Ethics* 1160a30–1161a9.
10. Regarding the four (or five) forms of democracy, see *Politics* 1291b30–1292a37, 1292b25–1293a10, as well as 1318b6.

induce a perception of human association as relatively homogeneous in its composition and, even more problematically, as a self-contained and self-referential environment: marked by forgetfulness of its nonhuman conditions, separated from what is above and what is below, from what precedes and what follows, from the source and what springs or sprouts from it. The humanity that resolves itself exclusively into horizontality, according to the figure of the fraternal bond, seems reluctant to question itself about its origin and about its end and aim, incapable of marvel at the past, at ancestral origin, as much as with respect to the future, to the energy of the present. In this passage, in fact, Aristotle's focus on the unequal, on asymmetrical relationships, seems to be a reminder of human procession from out of the nonhuman, of the human being's dependence on the nonhuman, be it nature or god. It reminds us of the human as natural or divine *offspring*.

The discussion of these relations in the *Eudemian Ethics* confirms, from the very beginning, our hypothesis. The introduction of the theme of friendship between unequals, as much on the political level (governing/governed) as on the familial level (parent/child), evokes with a certain immediacy relations that exceed the human domain (paradigmatically, the one between the human and the divine). Here, Aristotle resorts again to the language of excess, *hyperbole*, but in this case it is not so much a matter of the rapture and the imponderability of "perfect" friendship, but rather a matter of the extraordinary disparity of the relations under consideration. In these cases, the distance between those who are involved (and between their respective ways of loving) is unbridgeable to the point that reciprocity becomes inconceivable: not only incalculable (as was in the case with "perfect" friendship) but unthinkable. Illuminated in an exemplary way by the reference to the "love of the god for the human being," these friendships take place "according to excess," *kath' hyperbolen*: they traverse absolute discontinuity, establish a bond with what is radically alien.[11] They point, indeed, to a bond without measure.

But let us return to the *Nicomachean Ethics*. In considering the relation between sovereign and subjects, Aristotle notes,

> Such too is the friendship of a father toward his children (although it differs in the greatness of the good services; for he is the cause of their being, which seems to be the greatest good, and also of their nurture and education; these things apply to the ancestors as well); for the

---

11. Aristotle, *Eudemian Ethics* 1238b18–23.

relation of a father to his children, or of the ancestors to their descendants, or of a king to his subjects, by nature involves ruling. And these are friendships in virtue of superiority, and for this reason parents are honored, too. Consequently, also the just in these relations is not the same for the two parties, but is based on merit; for even friendship is like this.[12]

Here underlined is the archaic character of the parent or, in general, of the forebears with regard to their offspring and further descendants. The father and the predecessor are principles of government in the sense that they are the causes of the generation and of the becoming of what follows: they give origin and form. The community of brothers should be referred back to this primordial scene: only in this perspective could they be adequately understood and comprehensively understand themselves. Hence, in the development from a friendship that involves equality to a friendship that implies an extreme asymmetry, a critique of the restrictions of the horizontal relation is outlined. Moreover, the relation between adults and children (as well as, more generally, the vertical friendship) paradigmatically reveals friendship as a bond extending beyond the community of those who "have" reason—that is, the community of those who humanly partake in reason. It is a friendship that stretches out toward living beings not yet (fully) human, or (what is more noteworthy) not even on the verge of becoming human, beings that do not tend to the human because they follow other trajectories—gods and animals.

The relation between brothers, in its relatively self-enclosed character, tends to forget its own bonds with the other: to forget discrepancy, difference in its many manifestations, and each one's involvement in it. Above all, the bond between peers tends to sever itself from vertical relationality, thereby confining friends of this kind to the condition of orphans: children deprived of parents and ancestral provenance, of the disposition to become, themselves, parents, to sense in themselves the fecundity of the present. The forgetfulness of brothers, their absorption in the fraternal bond, reveals human beings uprooted from nature, cut off from contact with the numinous, deprived of origin and orientation. It reveals a humanity incapable even of facing the question concerning the dead and the unborn, the legacy it bears and the fruits it can bring forth, the beginning and the destination of the human species as such—that is, the situation of the human within the nonhuman (be it nature or

---

12. Aristotle, *Nicomachean Ethics* 1161a16–22.

divinity). In alluding to this limit in the love between equals, Aristotle encourages an interruption of horizontality: a love that would not remain "between us," but that would open itself infinitely to the infinite, to what cannot be horizontally embraced, what remains vertiginously excessive, impervious to reciprocation. In the end, the figure of asymmetrical relations favors a vision that overcomes the relations between human beings as such, and, for the same reason, relations that exclusively concern adult and rational men, thus manifesting the irreducibility of the human species to the community of those who are identical (brothers, peers, equally privileged citizens).[13] Hence, Aristotle points to the human within the nonhuman (gods and nature). This is the perspective of *sophia*, of human beings who look at the sky, who lift their gaze beyond their more immediate concerns, who find syntony and vision in this contact with a radiant nature or divinity.[14]

Wisdom is a contemplative practice that turns to the sky, and yet it does not sever the bond with the world and with the senses. It finds divinity within nature, hears the natural voice of the gods in the animation and the gleam of which the body of the cosmos vibrates. In this, the proximity of Aristotle and Plato is remarkable. Philo of Alexandria, Jewish Egyptian Neoplatonist (first century BC to first century AD), will observe that "those who practice wisdom, whether among the Greeks or the barbarians," seek to distance themselves not so much from the world as from the world of conventions, conveniences, and political calculation; "aspiring to a life in peace and serene, they contemplate in the best way nature and all that is therein; earth and sea, air and sky, and the various natures inhabiting them; they accompany the moon, sun, and the dance of the other stars, errant or fixed." And he concludes with the wondrous image of the human being in its duplicity, at once tree and bird: "Their bodies are indeed rooted below, but souls have wings, so that, crossing the air above, they may closely follow the powers dwelling there, as is fitting for those who have become citizens of the cosmos."[15]

In this way, too, friendship assumes the sense of a cosmic bond, in consonance with pre-socratic intuitions of various lineages (Pythagorean, Empedoclean), of which Platonists and Neoplatonists will later offer

---

13. Again, both the Platonic and the Aristotelian reading would demand a rigorous and minute confrontation with Derrida's *The Politics of Friendship*, trans. G. Collins (London: Verso, 1997).
14. Aristotle, *Nicomachean Ethics* 1141a35–b1.
15. Philo of Alexandria, *The Special Laws* 2.44–45.

their syntheses. Friendship, Iamblichus will say, "subsists in all things and toward all things."[16] Considerations concerning the *polis* as well as the *anthropos* must be situated within the context of such a vision of the *kosmos*. As Aristotle explains, the insistence on human genealogy is ultimately meant to puncture the exclusively human horizon: "The friendship of children toward their parents, and of human beings toward the gods, is a friendship toward the good and that which is superior; for parents have conferred the greatest good, since they are the causes of the being and nourishment of their offspring, and hence of their education."[17] At stake is not only the birth of children, but also the birth of humankind as such; not only the verticality of physiological procreation and the chain of generations, but also the verticality within which the human is interwoven; not only the origin understood as beginning, but also the origin understood as continuous support and guide, as informing principle dynamically at work. The focus on the figures of parents, ancestors, kings, and gods marks the urgency of the interrogation concerning human provenance and its environment.

The love from the higher being takes the form of a bestowal, of protection and support. In turn, the love from the more vulnerable being takes the form of a desire for the other and for belonging: desire to stretch out and extend beyond oneself, to embrace and be held, to be open to the other and by the other, to the point of becoming the bearer of the other. This structure of love on the part of the most vulnerable ones illustrates the condition of human beings with respect to what transcends them, to what constitutes their condition—in particular, with respect to the good, in its divinity and, together, its naturalness.[18] This love involves the desire that leads the individual out of itself, in a movement of yearning and receptivity.

We therefore find, in the folds of the incisive Aristotelian argumentation, cross-references and echoes of ancient teachings, even of Pythagorean register. It is rarely said, and so it is worth underlining—also in order to suggest that, in the repertoire of antiquity much remains to be thought through. We know that the phrase *philotes isotes*—that is, the conviction of the equality between friends—is attributed to Pythagoras. But Xenophanes also mentions an anecdote about Pythagoras: "They say that once, while he was passing by, a puppy was being beaten; he pitied

---

16. Iamblichus, *On the Pythagorean Way of Life*, 33.
17. Aristotle, *Nicomachean Ethics* 1162a4–7.
18. Aristotle, *Eudemian Ethics* 1249b14–15.

it and said: 'Stop, do not hurt it, this is the soul of someone who was my friend, I know it because I have heard the voice.'"[19] This is the capacity to sense life—literally, to hear its voice, its suffering, and to recognize its nearness, indeed, its equality—recognizing oneself in it, in full and sentient participation. This is the feeling of equality that unites well beyond equivalences and specular reciprocity: equality across unfathomable differences, and yet vivid, undeniable. Cicero will observe, in a lamentably fragmentary annotation, "Indeed, men who are not mediocre, but excellent and educated, Pythagoras and Empedocles, declare that one and the same is the condition of all living beings before the law, and that inexpiable penalties threaten those who do violence to an animal. It is a crime, then, to harm a beast, and this crime . . ."[20] So it is that the sharing of *pathos*, fragility, exposure to suffering, mortality, are shared in a form of cosmopolitanism that articulates itself neither only horizontally nor only vertically, but rather irradiates in every direction: once again, the solar dimension of friendship.[21]

We have, up till now, been reflecting from various angles on this word, "equality," always maintaining the commitment to a close listening of Aristotle. And we cannot deny the friendship (the consonance, the harmony, although at great distance) between his gaze and Pythagoras's ear.

COMMUNICATIONS

Through these diverse discourses on friendship (whose cohabitation is not always smooth) the figure of interdependence comes to be delineated. It emerges as much horizontally, in the relations within the human environment, as vertically, in human exchanges with the nonhuman. (Let us, however, recall the difficulty—if not the impossibility—of drawing and maintaining this distinction.) In the context of human relations and interactions, both within a *polis* and among *poleis*, the pervasiveness of dialectical practice sheds light on dialogue in its salient features: ongoing negotiation, exchange, and transmission; the work of connection, communion, and communication that animates togetherness. Certainly dialogue cannot be limited, in this sense, to a rhetorical duel or dispute,

---

19. Xenophanes, 7 Diels-Kranz.
20. Cicero, Marcus Tullius, *De re publica* III.11, 199–201.
21. One of the sentences collected by Matteo Ricci in *De amicitia* (1595), his first work in Chinese, reports the analogy between friendship, the sun lighting up the sky, and the eyes lighting up the body. Matteo Ricci, *On Friendship*, trans. Timothy Billings (New York: Columbia University Press, 2009), sentence #79.

but rather must be understood as a conversation whose premise and condition is the attitude of friendship. Nevertheless, since the phenomenon of interdependence is not confined within the human horizon, we are induced to consider more in depth the matter of communication, beyond strictly human conversation and language (or better: languages, *logoi*, always plural).

The course of the argumentation, in its allusive breadth and in its gashes, leads us to interrogate ourselves about the work of mediation, as patient as it is improbable—about our bearing toward environments other than the human, about the work of communication that exceeds human dialectic and that is always already underway, even if, for the most part, unconsciously. How can we begin to heed and to practice friendship's many languages—the languages, registers of communication and life, which can do justice to the bare fact of interdependence? In what way, other than ordering, arranging, pillaging, and objectifying, could we interact with what surrounds and contains us, with the forms of life around, above, and below us? How can we let what surrounds us traverse us and solicit us, how can we act so as to respond to, and correspond with, this reception? How, in other words, can action unfold out of undergoing, in response, responsibly?

Perhaps the answer to these questions has nothing do with repertoires of precepts. Aristotle limits himself (but he is tireless, in this) to underlining the importance of evaluations adhering to the ever unique traits of every situation, maintaining a living contact with things and, therefore, responding in the most sensible way to the issues each time in play. It is in this perceptual refinement, in this availability to following the wavering course of things, in this bond that does not imprison but, on the contrary, discloses, that we can reach a completely different kind of precision with respect to conceptual clarity and dialectical lucidity.

Amicable behavior is characterized by its tension toward the good: the friend wishes the good to the other, the good of the other, of others. They wish well, wish (for) the good and collaborate with it. But reckoning with circumstances so as to be guided by the overall end of being-well always involves bearing in mind the complexity of interactions, safeguarding them, holding them in care and attention, remaining aware of the entire relational and resonant context. Implicit in this posture is the sentiment of a rule of harmony and proportion governing the whole and the multiplicity that belongs to it. Responding to and corresponding with such a rule is, perhaps, what lies at the heart of friendship, broadly understood as an amorous and harmonizing relationality radiating in every direction. It is a rule that is sensed, not geometrically demonstrated: the friend, or the one who disposes oneself in a friendly way toward beings and things, knows this very well. Without definitions of the good and theorems on harmony, the friend senses the concreteness of the good, demands it concretely, and strives to contribute to its—infinite—manifestations.

9. SENSING-WITH

The "Other Things in Life"

Meditating on the friendship between excellent individuals, Aristotle has come to delineate the human being who soars beyond itself, caught in a movement of self-overcoming: the human being, precisely as human, as a figure of excess, and hence of opening and hospitality. In this sense, the human being properly (paradoxically) finds and recomposes itself only in projecting outside, in being beside itself, in the digression through the other. Even more radically, far from simply leading the other back to itself—far, too, from returning to itself as if the alienating egress were only an accidental deviation—in the mirror of the other the human being sees the trace of a further opening that cannot lead to any identity, the trace of a shared opening toward another who is neither another human being nor any other being. In the other who is the friend, one glimpses a shared opening to the good, an availability to it, for the love of it. In the affectionate impulse beyond itself, and in the diversion through the other, the individual discloses itself in terms of an infinite receptivity. Friendship encourages this.

It is in communal life that this being explicates itself in the amplitude of the possibilities that it keeps discovering in itself. As we have seen, this happens, paradigmatically, in the *polis*. Political life appears to be supremely choice-worthy, both because of the honor and glow inherent in public involvement, and because even activities of a contemplative character are only practicable thanks to the free time that political coexistence allows. Aristotle says, "The friendship between husband and wife seems to be by nature; for human beings by nature tend to form couples more than to be political, and they do this to the extent that a household is prior and more necessary than a *polis* and that reproduction is more common to animals. Accordingly, associations in the other animals exist only to that extent, but human beings live together not only for the sake of reproduction but for other things in life as well."[1] In and through life (living-together, sharing) in the *polis*, human beings can develop into what they are, realize their intrinsic potential—including the capacity for contemplation, thinking, imagination. Contemplation, let it be repeated again, is the activation of an absolutely salient human trait, and, at the same time, the activity in which the human is gathered, synthesized; Aristotle considers it the worthiest, most characteristic mode of human enactment. Of course, for him, intellectual activation is a certain kind of action: thought as such, "complete in itself" and aside from any practical application, is already in itself a practical matter, a matter of *praxis*.[2]

Hence, the "other things in life," which Aristotle hints at, presumably indicate the whole range of actions that, beyond reproduction and things pertaining to the "other animals," culminate in intellectual practice. One could say that Aristotle is here drawing on the "classical" contrast between *polis* and *physis*, between freedom and necessity, to underline how, in the *polis*, the human can distance itself from the encumbrances of animality (metabolic sustenance, reproduction, the labors of survival). Almost as if human beings could emancipate themselves from all that, and simply devote themselves to developing the faculties they harbor in virtue of having *logos*. The "other things in life" would then crucially designate the occupations of the citizen, participation in the construction of civic and civil life: the task of civilization. And yet, precisely at the apex of this long meditation on friendship, Aristotle surprisingly introduces, with force and determination unprecedented in this sphere, the animal. As we are about to see, he adds dimension to the sharing of life in the sense of *zoe*, in its perceptual and physical elements, drawing attention to that which remains unthought in a vitality that does not have the features of a *bios*. In the pleasure of shared sensory perception—of a staying together even without speaking, but "sensing together"—the "other

---

1. Aristotle, *Nicomachean Ethics* 1162a16–22.
2. Aristotle, *Politics* 1325b16–24.

things in life" have never before been so close to sweetness. Such a being together, as friends, is at once a politics realized in its sensible, lived, and unspoken ground, and a transgression of the *polis* by way of an excess both animal and divine. As we know from Aristotle himself, the animal and the god likewise fall outside the city.

Sweetness

Aristotle, then, brings the animal back into the center of political life. It is not enough to speak of embodied thought, which already is action in the world. Aristotle's gesture goes even further in indicating not only the unavoidability of sentient corporeality, but also and decisively the contact of above and below, of physical density and subtle perception: the most accomplished meditation, the most felicitous outcome of self-reflection, are inscribed in the animal. Immortality is, perhaps, precisely this: the capacity to "link together the beginning and the end," as Alcmaeon of Croton said.[3] Or: the capacity to divine the mutual belonging of the extremes. The passage at issue is unique for its delicateness and elation. It summons aesthetic refinement, the vividness and depth of *aisthesis* (in the translation of which I oscillate, no doubt improperly, between the language of sensation and that of feeling). It reveals the pleasure of *aisthesis* in its genuine philosophical scope—indeed, at the immovable center from which the discourses of philosophy move:

> Now, since living itself is good and sweet (and this seems to be the case since all desire it, and especially those who are good [ἐπιεκεῖς] and blessed; for it is to these that life [βίος] is most choice-worthy, and the most blessed life [ζωή] belongs to them), and since one who sees senses [αἰσθάνεται] that he or she sees, one who hears [senses] that he or she hears, one who walks [senses] that he or she walks, and similarly in the other cases, there is something in us which senses that we are in activity, and so we would be sensing that we are sensing and we would be thinking that we are thinking. But [to sense] that we are sensing or thinking [is to sense] that we are (for to be was stated to be sensing or thinking), and sensing that one lives is in itself one of the things which are pleasant (for life is by nature good, and to sense that the good belongs to oneself is sweet). Now living is choice-worthy, and especially by those who are good, since being to them is good and sweet (for they are pleased by sensing that which is in itself good).[4]

---

3. Aristotle, *Problems* 916a33.
4. Aristotle, *Nicomachean Ethics* 1170a27–1170b5.

Here, besides the often announced convergence of pleasure and happiness (that is, of the good), we note the intertwinement of the good and vitality. Vitality, being alive, means being in action, engaging in self-realization and fulfilment. The perception of such aliveness is good and indicates the good: one senses the good in sensing oneself alive.[5] But, above all, the Aristotelian language must be noted at this point: perceiving the good—that is, perceiving oneself in one's proper vitality—is, more precisely, a matter of sensing, *aisthanesthai*, in the middle voice, sensing oneself being or, better, resting in the sensation of being, in the movement of becoming, being the sensing. At play in the awareness of the good is the capacity of sensing oneself act, enact, of sensing one's own energy.[6] In other words, the awareness of the good is the sensing or feeling of life, the felt awareness that one is at work, in the unfolding of being—that one is, is there, in action. Let us note, too, that, differently from the passage considered above, in which being for the human being was intimated in terms of "thinking [νοῆσαι] and acting [πρᾶξαι],"[7] here it is said that "being is sensing or thinking," conferring an unexpected emphasis on sensuous perception, the deep and ultimate root of every *praxis* and (one would say) of thinking itself.

And again: this sentiment of harboring the good in virtue of the bare fact of being alive, the feeling of one's own living that turns back onto itself so as to feel itself, is more properly a sensing-together (*synaisthanesthai*): it discloses itself originarily in the proximity of the friend, in a being-with that senses itself as living-with, in the pleasantness of a feeling that is, hence, shared sensuousness, con-sent. Being is being alive and its good is sensing, feeling together, that one is, that one is-with: always already inscribed in being, is the community of sensing, of sensing-with, consenting—synesthetic politics. Aristotle continues,

> And if the good human being relates to him- or herself in the same way as he or she relates to the friend (for the friend is another self), then just as being is choice-worthy for everyone, so, or almost so, is the being of the friend. Being is choice-worthy because one senses one's own

---

5. In the preceding discussion on friendship, see 1166a11–29.

6. On the inseparability of the sensing and the sensed (sensing actualizes itself in the self-actualization of a being as sensed)—that is, on the concomitance of affection and activity—see *De anima* 425b26–426a12. On the reflexivity of sensation, and most basically of touch, C. Baracchi, "The Age of Distance: On an Ancient Hand Gesture," *Research in Phenomenology* 52, no. 2 (2022): 261–272.

7. Aristotle, *Nicomachean Ethics* 1155a16.

goodness [or because one senses that it is good], and this sensation is pleasant in itself. One must, therefore, sense-together [*synaisthanesthai*] the fact that the friend also is, and this happens in living-together [*syzen*] and sharing [*koinonein*] in discourses and thought. Hence it is said that human beings live-together and not that they simply feed in the same place, like cattle. If, then, being is in itself choice-worthy to someone blessed (for it is by its nature good and sweet), and if the being of the friend is almost equally choice-worthy, then the friend is one of the things to be chosen.... Hence, to be happy one needs good friends.[8]

Aristotle returns to this, significantly, with even greater clarity: "For friendship is a community [*koinonia*], and as one is toward oneself, so one is to the friend; in one's case the sensuous awareness [*aisthesis*] of existence is choice-worthy, and so therefore is that of the friend. But such a sensuous awareness becomes actual in living-together."[9]

In the good life, sensing the bare fact that one is, is pleasant (*hedy*): sweet, gratifying, delicately pleasing. This discloses friendship as the setting of a felicitous sharing, where defenses and resistances can be lowered, and one can simply be: be together, and sense oneself as well as the other, without predicates, definitions, or conceptual elaborations. This is the most fundamental ontology, already fully perceived in sensibility. Already fully co-sensed.[10] And since being seems originarily sensed jointly, since the sense of being arises out of co-sensing and consent, fundamental ontology is already politics: indeed, political action. It is therefore neither a matter of a contemplation leading back to discursive constructs—let alone rational ones—nor a matter of solitary contemplation. The most profound disclosure happens in these circumstances, not in an alleged withdrawal from the world and in an autonomous rational exercise (as if such things were even possible). Thus are intertwined, in the spacious hospitality of friendship, synesthesia, ontology, and politics. And a sweetness for which there is no further elaboration.

---

8. Aristotle, *Nicomachean Ethics* 1170b6–19.
9. Aristotle, *Nicomachean Ethics* 1171b33–35.
10. I borrow the translation of *synaisthanesthai* as "*con-sentire*" from Giorgio Agamben, *L'amico* (Rome: Nottetempo, 2007). This is an incisive reading of the passages we are considering here, even if Agamben inexplicably retains the distinction between being (essence, *quid est*) and existence (*quod est*), a distinction that has become historically necessary only since the sense of sensing disappeared, and along with it the fundamental ontology rooted in life.

Even reflexivity, self-reflective awareness and self-awareness (awareness aware of itself, awareness that lets the sense of the self-aware I emerge), far from (as they say today) "second order knowledge," gives itself at the aesthetic (synesthetic) level, at the level of (shared) sensory perception. It is not the apotheosis of abstract self-consciousness, but rather a reference back to itself through sensible routes. And it is precisely being together (with an other, with others) that makes me sense myself in turn: precisely while I feel the other's feeling and their sensible relation to themselves. I feel, sense-with, and I feel myself in the union with alterity, and never simply in an individual contemplative act that would be self-enclosed, separate, and abstract. Other, and otherwise than oversimplifying, is the simplicity of *synaisthanesthai*, of feeling together.

In this culminating moment of the reflection on friendship, then, is evoked the maximally accessible recomposition in the company of the friend, one's reunion with oneself through being-with and through recognition of the friend—a union that is characteristically given in the mode of sensing and therefore remains largely unspeakable (one senses that one senses, that one thinks, and hence that one is, that one is alive, and one senses it with joy, and further still senses that one is alive with another, with others, who also in turn live and sense themselves living . . .). So, here Aristotle points to the pleasure of this movement toward the one that remains not simple, to the recomposing and intrinsically therapeutic property of synesthetic awareness, to the saturated sweetness and exultation given in the intensification of coexistence by way of attention. This movement at once reflexive and ecstatic, this self-reflection by sensible routes, becomes possible with the friend, and actually fulfills itself in a consciousness (in an experience) clarified and stripped of words. It approaches the sense of being-there that can be tasted in meditative practices, where consciousness keeps company with the senses bright and alerted, and expands, finds boundless fulfillment in a gentle and sweet silence. In Vedic texts and in the Upanishads, and even in the Pāli canon, this pleasure is designated by the term *ananda*, even in the compound *sat-chit-ananda*. Sri Aurobindo, who, among other things, was an extremely refined scholar and polyglot, translates *ananda*, in English, as "delight": the delight that crosses all worlds, permeating all phenomena in constant variation; the delight of being (*sat*), gathered in consciousness (*chit*) and infinitely rejoicing in itself.[11]

---

11. Sri Aurobindo, *The Life Divine* (Pondicherry, India: Sri Aurobindo Ashram, 1970), in particular chapters 11, 12, and 23.

Noteworthy, finally, is the orienting role of pleasure: the arousal of pleasure as a symptom of being, of being in action, aimed at good and beautiful results—that is, happy. Aristotle observes that "living and pleasure appear to go together and not to admit separation; for there can be no pleasure without activity, and pleasure perfects every activity."[12] Pleasure crowns every act, marks the culminating moment in which the activity is accomplished. Any fulfillment of this kind would, by definition, be marked by pleasure. But Aristotle specifies, furthermore, that such pleasure should be understood as an excess of activity with respect to activity, as what would bring the activity beyond itself. This gesture intimates a different kind of completion, a different sense of the perfecting of an activity:

> (It is clear that pleasure arises with respect to each sensation, for we speak of sights and of things heard as being pleasant. It is also clear that these activities are most pleasant whenever both the sensation is at its best and its activity is directed toward its best corresponding object; and if both the object sensed and the one who senses it are such, there will always be pleasure provided both the one acting [ποιήσοντος] and that which is acted upon [πεισομένου] are present.) But pleasure perfects the activity not as a habit inhering in the one acting but as an end which supervenes like the bloom of youth to those in their prime of life.[13]

Pleasure is a completion that comes by itself, in a certain sense despite oneself: a completion that appropriates being in action in its unfolding, defining it further and drawing it into greater relief. Pleasure supervenes, overcomes, lifts the individual, frees the individual to delight. It comes, thus, to signify the beauty and the elation experienced in the activity that is fulfilled as if in and by itself, beyond effort, technique, expertise. Pleasure accompanies the work that releases itself, as a surplus altogether other than superfluous.[14]

At this point, Aristotle is making the transition from the discourse on friendship and its sweetness, to the detailed study of pleasure with which opens the final book of the *Nicomachean Ethics*. This book undertakes to examine the contemplative posture as the highest human act and as the highest good, for human beings and beyond. However, there

---

12. Aristotle, *Nicomachean Ethics* 1175a19–21.
13. Aristotle, *Nicomachean Ethics* 1174b27–34.
14. Aristotle, *Nicomachean Ethics* 1177a22–27.

is considerable fascination, as well as philosophical consequence, in the fact that Aristotle never leaves behind the focus on action, much less the world in which action unfolds. Even in its culminating moment, *theorein* does not seem to indicate a withdrawal from the world. On the contrary, contemplation (of being, of the world) is originary experience, primordially felt, radically preceding experience in the modern (empirical) sense, always already brought under the concept and thereby clarified. Pleasure is the surest sign of this meditative arrangement that is fulfilled in the world.

Aristotle insists with extreme determination on the fact that, on the one hand, this world provides the conditions for the possibility of contemplation, while, on the other, contemplation can optimally guide the worldly trajectory of an individual human being, and likewise a community. Contemplation and living-well—that is, the achievement of a certain harmony in action—if and when they happen, are far from happening separately.

Amicus Plato

It will then not be inappropriate, in conclusion, to observe that, even in these outcomes, Aristotle is not far from Plato the friend, although following a path all his own and of remarkable originality. As a final word on friendship, to speak of the life and of the worlds that friendship makes possible and authorizes, it will be sufficient to recall a passage from Letter VII. This is one of the very rare documents (held to be authentic, even if not with absolute certainty) in which Plato speaks in the first person. He says that the esoteric teachings are not doctrines to be imparted to a few, but rather incommunicable teachings, not translatable into discourse: teachings that can be learned only in living presence—that is, through experience, and necessarily together. Even in its sharp language, this passage is an homage to the sharing of life, to the living community that, alone, makes inquiry possible. Thanks to living-together, every researcher charts his or her own way; every researcher *is* the way:

> I know of certain others who have written on these same themes; but who they are, not even they themselves know. But this much I can say, about those who have written or intend to write, and presume they know the themes I am concerned with, saying they heard it from me, or from others, or that they discovered it by themselves: it cannot be, or so it seems to me, that these people know anything whatsoever about these matters. There is not, nor will there ever be, anything written by

me on this subject. For at stake is not anything that can be said, as are other teachings, but starting from being-together [*synousia*] for a long time, from a pursuit of the theme, and living-together [*syzen*], like a fire suddenly [*exaiphnes*] lit up, it is born in the soul and finds nourishment there.[15]

---

15. Plato, *Letter* VII 341b–d.

INDEX

abstraction, 5–6, 17, 24, 52, 80, 94, 108, 117, 136
action, 23–25, 31, 35, 57, 77, 129, 132–38
adversity, 1–2, 67. *See also* "dark times"
Aelred (of Rievaulx), 4
Agamben, Giorgio, 135n10
Alcestis, 73–75
Alcmaeon (of Croton), 133
antiquarian. *See* archaic
Apology (Plato's dialogue). *See* Plato
appearance, 44, 67, 112
appetite, 39. *See also* desire
archaic, 1–2, 43, 78, 112, 125
Aquinas, Thomas, 4, 78
Arendt, Hannah, 7, 10, 23
Aristotle, 3–4, 17–18, 58, 76–82, 113–15, 122; *De anima*, 134n6; *De caelo*, 123; *Eudemian Ethics*, 38, 52, 61, 81, 108–10, 123–24, 127; *Magna Moralia*, 58–59, 61; *Nicomachean Ethics*, 10, 17, 24, 30–35, 39–41, 46, 48–49, 53, 55–60, 76, 80–81, 103, 108–10, 114, 120–27, 132, 135–37; *Politics*, 51, 122, 126, 132; *Problems*, 133n3; *Protrepticus*, 122–23
Aristoxenus (of Tarentum), 32
Athens, 10, 64, 67, 70–71, 84, 90, 93
Augustine, 4, 56n52
Aurobindo, Sri, 136
authority, 67, 72, 94, 116
autarchy, 58, 61. *See also* autonomy
autonomy, 6, 38, 58, 61, 99, 115. *See also* individualism

Bacon, Francis, 4–5, 48
Bacon, Roger, 78

balance, 19, 49–50, 91, 93, 106, 114. *See also* moderation
barbarian, 95, 98–99, 126. *See also* foreigner
beautiful, 19, 31, 47, 73, 81, 89–90, 137
becoming, 2–3, 11, 14, 16, 23, 31, 35, 40–44, 51, 59, 78, 93, 115, 117, 125, 134. *See also* birth
belonging, 2–3, 11, 17–18, 23, 34, 36, 42–45, 76, 80, 98, 102, 108–9, 114, 117, 127, 133
beloved, 43, 54, 58, 73
beneficent. *See* benevolence
benevolence, 46, 49, 54–55, 107–10
Benveniste, Émile, 10, 21n40
birth, 14, 20, 62, 90, 127
Blanchot, Maurice, 80
brothers, 89, 120, 123–26. *See also* solidarity
borders, 75, 97–99
Bruno, Giordano, 17n31
Butler, Judith, 96n19

care, 15, 28–29, 31–33, 58, 78, 99–101, 129
celestial, 9–10, 12, 116
change, 12, 19, 73
children, 56, 96, 113, 124–27
Christianity, 4, 6, 28
Cicero, 3–4, 17n32, 32, 51n43, 128
citizens, 34, 42–43, 91, 95–98, 113, 120, 126. *See also* stateless
civilization, 132. *See also* culture
Cleanthes (of Assos), 116
collective, 3, 64, 98, 104, 108
common, 17, 29, 35, 37, 39–41, 45, 49, 77–79, 104–21 *passim*, 132

141

communication, 128–29. See also dialogue
community, 6, 11, 17–20, 35, 37, 42, 46, 54, 63–67, 71–74, 86–88, 90–91, 94, 97, 101, 104–6, 109, 111, 113, 116–23, 125–26, 128, 134–35, 138
consciousness, 16, 33, 68, 96, 111, 136
consensus, 86
constitution, 36, 60, 88, 98–99, 104–5, 111, 113
contemplation (theoria), 16, 25–27, 53, 69, 76, 79, 84, 89–90, 102, 122, 132, 135, 138. See also theory
contemporary, 2, 36
continence, 28. See also moderation
cosmos (kosmos), 12–16, 19–20, 24, 30, 62, 126
courage, 1, 26, 61, 73, 97
critique, 45, 66, 68, 78, 92, 99, 112, 125
culture, 6, 117
customs, 2, 10, 20, 71–74, 98, 112

"dark times," 36
death. See mortality
Deleuze, Gilles, 43n26
delight, 18, 20, 30, 56, 70, 136–37
democracy, 67, 112, 123
Derrida, Jacques, 112n18, 116, 126n13
desire, 14, 25–28, 39–43, 50, 57–58, 74–75, 79, 85, 91–94, 97, 100, 110, 118n26, 127, 133
dialogue, 71, 81, 93, 102, 128–29; Platonic dialogue, 107n4; dialogues of Plato (see Plato)
difference, 19–20, 23, 25–26, 28, 40, 61, 98, 117, 125. See also plurality
Diogenes Laertius, 40n24, 51, 116n24
divinity, 16, 33, 126–27. See also god/God
dogmatic, 2, 26, 27n8, 79
dreams, 35, 100–101
dynamics, 46, 59, 88, 92, 100, 104, 108n4

earth (Gaia), 3, 14–16, 126
economy, 34, 45

education, 5, 94, 97, 124, 127
egoism, 6, 109
embodiment, 54, 96
emotions, 5, 97
empathy, 5
Empedocles, 9, 21n42, 70n25, 128
Enlightenment, the, 116
enemy, 10–11, 19, 32, 63, 83–84, 88, 95–97, 111–12. See also enmity
enmity, 1, 11, 19, 84, 95–113 passim
environment, 5, 106, 124, 127–28
ephemeral, 9, 56, 121
epic, 65, 71. See also Homer
Epictetus, 116
Epicurus, 3, 61
equality, 5, 20, 40–43, 57, 117, 119–20, 125–28
eros, 21, 28, 49, 73–74, 106–7
erotic. See eros
Euripides, 2n2
evil, 57, 97
excellence, 26–31 passim, 34–35, 38, 41, 43, 47–49, 51, 53, 55–59, 66, 73–74, 81, 90, 110. See also virtue
excess, 39, 43, 49–50, 54, 58, 60, 74, 88, 91–92, 107, 114, 124, 131–33, 137
exclusion, 19, 44, 77, 117
existence, 63, 135. See also life
experience, 2, 5–6, 16–17, 31, 39, 52, 69–70, 79, 105, 117, 138. See also suffering

fact, 51, 86 (see also truth); factuality, 106
fidelity, 1, 32, 37, 78–80
foreigner (xenos), 11–12, 64, 83, 95
fragility, 17, 128
fraternity, 4, 112n18, 123. See also brothers
freedom, 3, 33, 36–37, 45, 67, 74, 78, 94, 109, 116–17, 132
Freud, Sigmund, 5–6, 29
friendship: instrumental friendship, 1, 22, 107; perfect friendship, 35, 41, 46, 49, 53, 56–57, 107–10, 114, 119, 124; philosophers' friendship, 52, 76–77,

79–80, 100; political friendship, 108–11, 113–14

Gadamer, Hans-Georg, 61n67
gender, 4. *See also* men, women
god/God, 2, 12, 21, 37, 56, 61, 64, 116, 122–24, 133 (*see also* divinity); gods, 14, 61, 66, 69, 73–74, 88, 120, 122, 125–27
gratitude, 92
Greek (ancient), 6
Guattari, Félix, 43n26
Guerlac, Henry, 79n6
guest, 11–12, 33. *See also* foreigner
guilt, 62. *See also* responsibility

Habermas, Jürgen, 116
happiness, 34, 37, 40, 60, 70–71, 105, 114–15, 134. *See also* joy, well-being
harmony, 19, 28, 60, 88, 91, 128–30, 138
hatred, 9. *See also* enmity
hearing, 9, 16, 66, 70
heavens, 123. *See also* celestial
Hegel, G. W. F., 67–68
Heraclitus, 12n15, 17, 116
Hesiod, 16n29, 21n43, 69
history, 72, 117
Homer, 32n5, 44–45, 69, 71, 77; *Iliad*, 32, 44, 71; *Odyssey*, 32n5, 44n28
hospitality, 10–11, 20, 39, 131, 135
host. *See* hospitality
household (*oikos*), 132
humanity, 4, 23, 33, 53, 71, 75, 86, 88, 96–97, 124–25; human rights, 5. *See also* hospitality
Hyginus, 35

Iamblichus, 32, 59n59, 127
ideas, 63, 76–77, 81–82, 92, 102
identity, 10, 38, 43, 45, 64, 92, 98, 111–12, 117–18, 122–23, 131
ideology, 110, 113
imagination, 106, 115, 117, 132
immutable, 100
implication, 88, 114. *See also* responsibility

impulse, 25, 39, 41, 49, 59, 63, 79, 87, 92, 100–101, 110, 131
individualism, 6, 36, 42, 117
infinity, 49
injustice, 67, 85, 96
institutions, 20, 63, 71, 105
integrity, 15, 26, 29, 53, 59
interdependence, 20, 65, 82, 87, 105–6, 114, 128–29
interpretation, 45, 95, 111
intimacy, 1, 10–11, 20, 40, 52, 74, 80, 96n19, 104
isolation. *See* solitude

joy, 20, 33, 52, 59, 92
judgment, 78
Jung, Carl Gustav, 29n12
justice, 3, 18, 20, 26, 28–29, 41, 48, 67, 80, 83–85, 89, 103–5, 108, 112, 114, 129

Kant, Immanuel, 5, 37, 115–16
Kristeva, Julia, 96n19, 116

law, 103, 160, 163–64, 166–67, 171, 183
liberalism, 5
life, 4, 7, 9, 12–18, 24–26, 31–35, 37–38, 52–54, 62–65, 67–69, 73–74, 81, 86–90, 93, 101–5, 114, 118, 130–33; communal life, 46, 131; forms of life, 45, 116, 128–29; good life, 29–30, 135; human life, 49; as a whole, 121–22
light, 9–12, 19, 26, 32, 44, 63, 81–83, 90, 100. *See also* sight
limits, 42, 49, 52–53, 61, 97–98, 112, 116, 123
Locke, John, 5
love, 3–5, 38, 45–46, 49, 51, 54–61, 72–74, 89–90, 93–95, 100–101, 106–7, 126–27, 131 (*see also* eros); of the good, 29, 39, 43, 60; Lucretius, 21n42; of truth, 76–79

maturity, 67
McCarthy, Mary, 7
mean (*mesotes*), 106. *See also* moderation
meaning, 45, 68, 121

memory, 17, 19, 63, 87
men, 42, 62, 64, 67–74, 77–79, 94–96, 113, 126–8
microcosm, 21, 109. *See also* cosmos
Mill, John Stuart, 72
moderation, 26, 74
modernity, 5, 36, 84
Montaigne, Michel de, 4, 50–51, 71–2
moralism, 4, 27n8, 37
mortality, 15, 92, 113, 128
mother, 56, 66, 73
multiplicity, 25, 49, 74, 118, 129. *See also* plurality
multitude, 21, 24, 65, 116
myth, 19, 22–23, 67, 86, 102n29, 113. *See also* story

Nancy, Jean-Luc, 116
Narcissus, 22
narrative, 10, 86
nationalism, 117
nature, 5–6, 11, 20, 36, 48–49, 73, 85–86, 91–92, 109, 116, 120–26, 132–35
necessity, 8, 20, 30–34, 65, 67, 87, 92, 94, 99, 106, 111, 132
Nehamas, Alexander, 110n10
Neoplatonists, 126. *See also* Platonism
Neumann, Erich, 29n12
New York, 92
Nietzsche, Friedrich, 5, 27n8, 39, 64n3, 72
normativity, 105, 107
novelty, 19, 92

objectivity, 61, 94
ontology, 135
opinion, 50, 53, 78, 86, 96, 112
originality, 138

parent(s), 73, 120, 124–25, 127
Parmenides, 21n41
passion, 25, 27, 50, 57, 67, 70, 79, 94
peace, 29, 47, 88, 91, 93–94, 126
perfection, 13, 19, 34–35, 47, 54, 61, 105, 114, 119–20
person, 47, 54, 62, 68, 134

perspective, 3–4, 6, 17, 36, 41, 76, 85, 106, 109, 111, 117, 120–21, 125–6
Phaedrus (Plato's dialogue). *See* Plato
phenomenology, 3, 110, 119
Philebus (Plato's dialogue). *See* Plato
philosophers, 52, 76–80, 100
philosophy, 62–63, 66, 68, 77, 80, 89, 94–95, 99, 133
planet, 55. *See also* world; earth
Plato, 3–4, 10, 19, 25, 27, 39, 49, 72, 76–80, 90, 92, 126, 138–9; *Apology*, 31n4, 62–64, 66–70; *Letter VII*, 52n46, 90, 138–39; *Phaedrus*, 17n32, 20n39, 28, 33, 61, 64, 70, 73–74, 94, 107n4; *Philebus*, 81; *Republic*, 18–19, 24, 26–28, 39, 59, 65, 67, 69, 77, 81–86, 88–102 *passim*, 106, 111–13; *Sophist*, 63–64; *Symposium*, 20, 33, 69, 73, 89–90, 99, 107n4, 118n26; *Timaeus*, 9–16, 19, 28
Platonism, 80
Plautus, 4
play, 19, 29, 77, 107, 129
pleasure, 6, 30, 33–34, 37, 54–56, 107, 121, 132–34, 136–37
plurality, 23, 53, 74, 106
polis, 18, 20, 23, 25, 27, 46, 64–65, 71, 83, 85–86, 88–100, 103–5, 109, 111, 114, 121–22, 127–28, 131–33
political, 3, 5, 10, 20, 36, 42, 56, 74, 108–10, 114–16, 121, 132–33; political organism, 97, 112–13 (*see also* life); political space, 23, 88, 111, 113
Porphyry, 59
poverty, 88
power, 2, 27–28, 42, 53, 67–68, 72, 81, 100, 120, 123
practice (*praxis*), 23, 66, 132, 134
precariousness, 17, 96
prejudice, 8, 91
private, 5, 72, 104, 109–10, 115
production, 92, 114
promise, 105
property, 17, 38, 118
potentiality, 24, 31–32, 53, 77, 99, 107

Pythagoras, 17n32, 32, 40, 59, 122, 127–28

race, 117
rationality, 90, 116–17. *See also* reason
reason, 28, 31, 48, 90, 99–100, 115–18, 125
receptivity, 39, 57, 77, 127, 131
recognition, 5, 12, 42, 98, 108–9, 111, 119, 121, 136
relation, 5, 11, 20, 24, 36, 42, 45–49, 51–52, 56, 58–62, 78, 80, 110, 120–25, 136
reproduction, 132
Republic (Plato's dialogue). *See* Plato
resistance, 90, 135
responsibility, 78
revolutionary, 24, 67–68
Ricci, Matteo, 128n21
Rohde, Erwin, 93n15
Rousseau, Jean-Jacques, 5

Sallis, John, 13n17, 99n23
sameness, 113. *See also* identity
Schmitt, Carl, 111–14 *passim*
selfishness, 5. *See also* individualism
self-sufficiency, 59, 87. *See also* autonomy
sensation, 9, 33, 133–35, 137. *See also* hearing, sight, taste, touch, vision
sight, 9–10, 16, 18, 27, 54, 82, 101, 137. *See also* vision
significance, 5, 115, 123. *See also* meaning
Sinaiko, Hermann, 99n23
singularity, 2, 6, 36, 42, 62, 107, 115, 118. *See also* individualism
"social contract," 86
society, 1, 5, 72
Socrates, 10, 63–75, 77–78, 81, 84–91, 93–102, 111
solidarity, 2–3, 6, 11, 18, 20, 30, 83, 86, 91, 104, 111, 114, 120. *See also* friendship; political
solitude, 4, 23, 25
Solon, 12
Sophist (Plato's dialogue). *See* Plato
sophists, 64
soul (*psyche*), 13, 25–27, 35, 51–52, 62, 83, 86, 112

speech, 23, 35, 63–64. *See also* dialogue
Speusippus, 76
stateless, 64
Stoics, 116
story, 10, 12, 20, 62, 72–73, 84, 102. *See also* myth
study, 24, 49, 137. *See also* contemplation
subjectivity, 116. *See also* individualism
suffering (*pathos*), 9, 13, 52, 61, 85, 89, 106, 117, 128
survival, 31, 33, 63, 92, 105, 132
Symposium (Plato's dialogue). *See* Plato

Tarán, Leonardo, 79n6
taste, 9
theater, 10, 14, 23, 63–64, 122
Theognis (of Megara), 1–2
theory, 88, 116. *See also* contemplation
therapy, 33, 89, 93, 100
thinking, 16–17, 22, 42, 51, 70, 80, 83–84, 104, 109–10, 113–15, 132–34. *See also* contemplation
Timaeus (Plato's dialogue). *See* Plato
touch, 9, 16, 84, 116, 134n6
tradition, 2, 65, 71, 116
truth, 19, 50, 71, 77–79, 82, 101, 117
tyranny, 83, 100, 123

understanding, 18, 24, 29, 45, 57, 70, 83, 96, 104, 117–18
unity, 9, 25–28, 53, 98, 108
utopian, 30

Valerius Maximus, 33n7
violence, 35n14, 86–87, 106, 128
virtue, 31, 35, 39, 41, 45, 48, 59, 73, 79, 81, 83, 94, 107, 134. *See also* excellence
vision, 4–6, 19, 23, 25–27, 32–33, 42, 62, 70–71, 86, 101–2, 105, 114–16, 126–27. *See also* sight
vulnerability, 130, 133

war, 1, 29, 32, 84, 86–88, 91–92, 94, 96–98, 100, 102, 111–13, 121
Warburg, Aby, 74

Weil, Simone, 8n1, 28n11, 116
well-being, 33n7
wickedness, 57
Wilde, Oscar, 36
withdrawal (from the world), 90, 135, 138
women, 42, 62, 68–73 *passim*, 94, 96, 113
wonder, 11–12, 16, 24, 32
Woolf, Virginia, 72n31
work, 12–13, 17, 28, 35, 50, 55, 68, 71, 127–29, 134, 137
world, 3–4, 8–10, 12–17, 21–24, 27, 31, 33, 36, 45, 60, 64–65, 68, 70, 80, 83, 89–90, 93, 95, 98–99, 109, 116, 120, 122–23, 126, 133, 135, 138

Xenocrates, 76
Xenophanes, 127–28
Xenophon, 63

youth. *See* children

Zeno (of Citium), 116
Zeus, 44, 116

CLAUDIA BARACCHI is Professor of Moral Philosophy at the Università di Milano-Bicocca. She is the author of *Of Myth, Life, and War in Plato's Republic* (2002), *Ethics as First Philosophy* (2008), *L'architettura dell'umano. Aristotele e l'etica come filosofia prima* (2014), and *Il cosmo della Bildung* (with R. Rizzi, 2016), among others. She is a practicing analyst in Milan.

FOR INDIANA UNIVERSITY PRESS

Emily Baugh, *Editorial Assistant*
Brian Carroll, *Rights Manager*
Gary Dunham, *Acquisitions Editor and Director*
Anna Francis, *Assistant Acquisitions Editor*
Brenna Hosman, *Production Coordinator*
Katie Huggins, *Production Manager*
Darja Malcolm-Clarke, *Project Manager and Editor*
Dan Pyle, *Online Publishing Manager*
Leyla Salamova, *Artist and Book Designer*
Stephen Williams, *Marketing and Publicity Manager*

www.ingramcontent.com/pod-product-compliance
Lightning Source LLC
Chambersburg PA
CBHW030656230426
43665CB00011B/1124